HOW TO BE A
BADASS

NAVIGATING
YOUR ROAD TO
SELF-MASTERY

NIKKI LANGMAN

Cover design: Ultimate World Publishing
Layout and typesetting: Ultimate World Publishing
Editor: Emily Riches
Cover image: Izf/shutterstock.com

Ultimate World Publishing
Diamond Creek,
Victoria Australia 3089
www.writeabook.com.au

TESTIMONIALS

"Through her personal story Nikki helps us see and understand ourselves more deeply. Then through her BADASS framework she gives us a powerful road map for improving our wellbeing and being more of our best self, more often. Her story is inspirational and the framework is powerfully simple and practical to apply. It's an exceptional read for anyone, either at the beginning of their own journey, or experienced on the path to self-mastery."

Dr. Ben Palmer
Chief Executive Officer
Genos International

"If you need some motivation or encouragement on your journey towards self-mastery, then dive right into *How to be a BADASS*. Nikki's story is raw yet hopeful, and her courage and brutal honesty are nothing short of inspirational."

S.C. Farrow
Author of *This is Not a Lie* and *Open Wounds*

"This was exactly what I needed right now to repave my road to being my most powerful self. Nikki Langman's ability to open up her readers' minds and hearts to honestly reflect on their own lives as they read about her personal journey is transformational. Her perspective on the internal battles we have within ourselves is deeply honest and challenges you to find a space to overcome what's rooted inside. The BADASS framework is a relatable formula that is applicable in every aspect of life and once understood and adopted, can be a lifelong guide."

Lori Namazi
Founder and CEO
Namazi Real Estate Resources

"We learn from our successes but we learn more from our failures and overcoming obstacles. Nikki Langman has had great experience in all three of these areas. Put her on your list under admiration and inspiration and read this book."

Simon Madden
Modern Business Coach and High-Performance
Consultant

"You know when you come across a true story that gets under your skin and you can't put it down? Nikki Langman has one you can't ignore. I admire her grit and tenacity, her honesty and heart – Nikki is one of my heroes and don't we all need one right now!

How to be a BADASS is a must-read and it will become your honored companion. Nikki's story is riveting and inspirational with gripping rawness and transformation that is powerfully motivational. The framework is practical with transferrable guidelines and a thought-provoking formula for success. This book will show you how to be BADASS every day – the world needs you to!"

Carrie Benedet
Human-Centered Coach and EI Specialist
Cultural and Wellbeing Sustainability in Education
Certified Facilitator

"This is a book that will inspire, empower, and encourage anyone who reads it. It is a raw, authentic, and honest account of Nikki's journey through struggle and anguish to acceptance and, ultimately, celebration of her whole self.

It is a story about what becomes possible when we allow ourselves to identify, accept, and step into our own power.

It is a reminder that we are not defined by our accomplishments, and that the greatest gift we can offer to the world is our truest and most integrated selves. This is only possible when we embrace and honor our story: even the darkest and prickliest bits.

Written from the heart, with courage, candor, and wit, this book will simultaneously make you want to be a better you, and show you how to do it. It is a must-read. The more badasses in the world, the better it will be for all of us."

Kate Witteveen
Success and Empowerment Coach
Author of *Why Being Good Can be Bad for You*

"Nikki's story about addiction is one that is so authentically raw and insightful. She takes us on her personal journey and you simply do not want to stop reading; apprehensive about what is coming next. Nikki writes with complete candor and shows us the heartbreaking reality of this ugly, oftentimes all-consuming disease. Her bravery shines through and she teaches us about the value of self-love. The BADASS framework is easily applicable to so many situations that many of us go through in life.

This is a book that will stay with you for a long time and one that you will refer back to time and time again. A true testament of resilience and motivation. Nikki is a brilliantly talented woman."

Sabrina Rojas
Motivational Speaker
Author of *Oh Sh*t!!! I Have Cancer*

"A REAL story for REAL people with REAL action steps for being your best self. Nikki is an inspiration – her candid, genuine, and practical BADASS framework enables all of us to identify who we really are and what our values are – realizing and unleashing our potential and learning how to manage our thoughts and emotions for productive relationships.

Nikki's sharing of her powerful journey enables us to get BADASS results in all aspects of our lives. Thank you, Nikki!"

Debbie Muno
Managing Director
Genos North America

"Drawing on personal life experiences, Nikki demonstrates the potential for any person to be 'powerfully extraordinary' just as she has become, regardless of the adversities and challenges we all face. It is packed with great insights into how to transform your life and how to do it like a badass! If you're looking for emotionally intelligent and inspiring motivation, or simply need hope, you must read this empowering book."

Shelley Maree Hunter
Wellness and Wellbeing Coach
Author of *Face of Faith*

"Nikki is a hero among heroes! This book is a reflection of her honesty, her truth, and her journey to self-mastery – yet it's so much more. Each page is filled with powerful, inspirational, and motivational insights – not only from her amazing story but from her incredible BADASS framework that, when implemented, will miraculously change your life forever.

Nikki inspires you to become the best version of yourself no matter what circumstance or situation you may find yourself in. This book is an epic roadmap leading you to unlimited physical, mental, and emotional potential, overcoming limiting beliefs, and propelling you forward to live a phenomenal life beyond your imagination."

Taloa Walters
Author of *Spirit Freedom*

"Nikki Langman is a BADASS in a most unique way! This book will lead you through her raw and personal journey, from the depths of despair through to success – sharing her learnings, strategies and very practical tips along the way.

This book will connect with a range of people from those wanting to enhance their effectiveness at work to those wanting to improve their performance on the sports field; from those experiencing life challenges to those suffering addictions – and many more.

Nikki speaks from real-life, lived experience and tells it like it is. This book will stimulate self-reflection, thought, and change you for the better. Thank you, Nikki, for your bravery in sharing your BADASS journey. This book will help many people."

Jayne Arlett
Small Business Consultant
Author of *Big Little Business*

DEDICATION

To my dad, who never let go.

CONTENTS

INTRODUCTION

When we look at someone we care about, it's easy to see how amazing they are. We see their strengths and gifts and know that they can do anything they set their mind to and overcome any challenges they might face. From the outside, their potential is effortless for us to grasp. But when we look at ourselves, we don't trust that we have the same potential. When it's our own capability or struggle that we are assessing, our perspective is remarkably different.

There is a parable about a man who was walking through a village one day and passed by a small group of elephants. He suddenly stopped, confused by the fact that these huge creatures were being held by one small rope tied to their front leg. No chains or cages, just a flimsy rope. It was obvious that the elephants could, at any time, break away from the ropes they were tied to but for some reason, they did not. The man saw a trainer nearby and asked why these magnificent animals just stood there and made no attempt to get away.

"Well," the trainer said, "when they are very young and much smaller, we use the same size rope to tie them and, at that age, it's enough to hold them. As they grow up, they are conditioned to believe they cannot break away. They believe the rope can still hold them, so they never try to free themselves." The man was amazed. These animals could at any time release themselves from their bonds but because they believed they couldn't, they were trapped in the same spot.

The man gazed in wonder at one of the biggest female elephants. The elephant is one of the most robust animals on earth, but she can be effectively confined by one thin rope and a lot of adaptation. The rope is weak and with one forceful kick of her leg, the mighty beast would be free. But in her mind, the rope is indestructible. When she was small, she tried to break the rope several times, but she couldn't. She had no idea how powerful she would become and what she would one day be capable of. That little rope was once too much to overcome, so she stopped trying. She stopped believing in her strength.

This is a powerful metaphor for the influence of the human mind. Like the elephants, how many "ropes" do you have holding you back? How many of your goals, talents, and challenges are bound in your mental ropes? How many beliefs are you holding onto that you can't do something, simply because at one point it was too difficult for you, or you failed at it once so now you don't even try?

If a puny rope was tied to your friend's foot, keeping them from moving, you'd tell them to cut it off. But what about when it's tied to your foot, tripping you every time you try to step forward? Do you notice it, or have you just resigned to it being a part of who you are? Over time, we can begin to think that we are not suited to do a particular thing and we accept this as the truth and limit ourselves to a discouragingly restricted world.

The fibers of our ropes are often made up of our limiting beliefs that we aren't good enough, strong enough, or worthy enough. The ropes are woven with the shame we feel for our mistakes, our failures, and our regrets. The ropes begin to feel tremendously heavy over time as more experiences strengthen the ropes in our minds. We lose faith in our ability to ever move forward and we develop a distorted perception of our own strength. Think about it for a moment: a full-grown elephant could rip an entire tree trunk out of the ground with a bit of effort, let alone snap a tiny rope. What if our ropes are just as easy to defeat?

Just like the growing elephant, we adjust to our surroundings and live within our perceived limitations. But we can also change our beliefs of what we are capable of and explore different possibilities. There might be a rope around you, but what you choose to believe about that rope is what matters. You might discover that you are much more powerful than you ever thought you were.

This book is written in two parts. The first part is my personal journey. It highlights some of my experience with the ropes that bound me to over 30 years of addiction and how I finally broke out of my own captivity. Once I set myself free and began to explore my own power, I tapped into abilities I didn't know I had. I share my story of venturing into the sport of endurance running at the age of 40 and going from zero athletic experience to running my first ultramarathon in just over two years. I achieved that, not by discovering some hidden physical talent, but by completely making over my mindset of what I was capable of and destroying my limiting beliefs. I don't tell my story to encourage sympathy or boast about triumph, but to demonstrate how an ordinary person can do extraordinary things by simply believing in their own potential and not giving up on themselves.

The second part of the book is the BADASS framework that I developed along my journey. The framework is my answer to the question that I have been exploring for several years: *What does it take to become your most powerful self?*

The BADASS model comprises years of my professional work and study – research, observation, learning, coaching, mentoring, teaching – life experience, and a lot of trial and error. The framework is an acronym (B = Brave, A = Authentic, D = Direction, A = Action, S = Self-love, and S = Self-talk). Each letter of the acronym has a dedicated chapter that demonstrates how you can incorporate that competency into your life to become your most powerful self in all that you do. In whatever way we approach life and all of its messiness, the road to self-mastery takes some pretty badass actions to be successful in the long run.

As you navigate your road to self-mastery, *be BADASS every day.*

"Knowing others is intelligence; knowing yourself is true wisdom.

Mastering others is strength; mastering yourself is true power."

— **Lao Tzu**

PART ONE

THE JOURNEY WITHIN

CHAPTER ONE

DIGGING DITCHES

I am not done yet. That is the one and only certainty I have about my life.

Today, I am at peace with my purpose. I have solid confidence in where I am going and what I feel called to achieve and, the more action I take in that direction, the more my vision crystallizes. Clarity didn't happen overnight though and I have spent a lot of time probing the big questions and trying in vain to "figure it all out."

Why are we here? Or in my case, why am I *still* here? That was my big question and I have come to accept ambiguity. I will never know for sure, but I am satisfied with this for now: my God isn't finished with me yet. I wholly believe this to be true because I thought my life would have ended a long time ago. I spent many years (until my mid-30s actually) resigned to a belief that I would die young, by my own accidental hand; a miscalculation of dosages or combination of substances that one day my body would just no longer handle… and that would be it. Game over. I surrendered to the idea that my legacy would be nothing more than a statistic, a tragic shame, another life taken way too young.

I kept this notion that I was destined to die young zipped tightly to myself because I was terrified that if I actually spoke those words, I would somehow inadvertently spark a cosmic reaction that would make the event come true. I also didn't want anyone to know that I assumed I would die prematurely by overdose for fear that my loved ones would coerce me into changing my reckless behavior and I wasn't interested in that option. So, I kept my undercurrent of thoughts private – that any day might be my last and I was powerless to change that. Those are some pretty powerful chains to bind yourself in.

THE GIN SOLUTION

My relationship with alcohol started exceptionally young. I was seven years old the first time I remember an upsetting event happening ("problem") and turning to alcohol for comfort ("solution"). It was learned behavior, for sure. I remember noting that after my parents would argue, which was frequently, my dad would go and fix himself a martini in his bar and drink it alone while he licked his emotional wounds. I don't ever recall my father exhibiting what I consider alcoholic behavior: he was always controlled about when and how much he drank. But I observed enough at home to make the connection that when you were feeling negative emotions, a drink would fix it. My parents were big entertainers with regular poker nights and some bizarrely themed parties so we had a fully stocked bar with just about every type of liquor you could imagine at all times. There was never a shortage of alcohol around our home.

One unremarkable day when I was seven, I was disturbed by something that occurred at school. I have no recollection of what took place, but it must have been hurtful enough for me to experiment with Dad's martini trick.

That night after everyone went to bed, I snuck into the bar and took a water glass and filled it about three-quarters full with gin. No mixers or ice, just straight gin. I obviously hadn't paid attention to the specifics of how you were supposed to prepare an alcoholic drink. It might have looked suspicious if I sat across the bar from my dad and took notes, I suppose. But my logic told me that gin was clear and clear drinks go in water glasses. I choked down the whole glass in about seven big gulps. It was the most terrible thing I had ever tasted or smelled; it reminded me of a Christmas tree. My flesh and esophagus felt like it was blistering and I wanted to cough and cry out, but I certainly didn't want to wake my parents up and get caught, so I suffered with silent tears streaming down my face as the fire of gin consumed my quivering body. I could not comprehend why this made Dad feel better when he was sad.

I was just about to rule this idea out completely when something marvelous happened. The burning sensation and body aches melted away and I felt a warming sensation like a cozy blanket begin to wash over me. Now this... this was cool. I liked the snuggly fleece feeling. That made sense to me. I always felt comforted by my teddy bear or a soft blanket and I didn't see adults hugging stuffed toys, so drinking alcohol must be the way they felt safe. The glass was empty and my head started to spin. I didn't have the understanding at that time that I had consumed a pretty large amount of spirits, but I did have the awareness that my physical sensations were changing rapidly and I better get the heck out of there and under my covers quickly. I cleaned the water glass and refilled the gin bottle from the tap and somehow managed to get back into my bedroom. I don't remember the walk or crawl down the hall. I was probably starting to black out at that point.

A little while later, I woke up violently vomiting all over my bed and the carpet. It was no longer an option to stay quiet and my mother came rushing in. I'm sure she was overwhelmed by the stench of gin immediately, and out of fear of my father waking up and learning what I had done, she frantically worked to strip the bed sheets, keep my sobs muffled, and make sure I was going to be okay. She and I never spoke about that incident again. I don't think my mother ever told anyone else about that night either, and certainly not my dad. It must have terrified and confused her as to why her seven-year-old daughter would sneak alcohol in the middle of the night. Perhaps she was hoping that I had learned my lesson and that she could erase it from her mind, too.

I don't know how I escaped alcohol poisoning that night. I don't have the medical knowledge to analyze that event, but I believe the physical consequences could have been much worse than they actually were. Many years later I would recall my father often expressing in exasperation, "Nikki always lands on her feet." Meaning that I repeatedly seemed to escape bad situations unscathed, where severe consequences or harm to myself or others could have easily been a factor. Looking back, that "cloak of protection" was there from day one.

You'd hope that most people, especially a child, would learn from an experience like that and it would put them off of alcohol completely until they were much older. But not me. Getting sick wasn't nice nor were the aftereffects the next day (the word "hangover" wasn't a part of my vocabulary yet), but I was a tough little soldier and was willing to accept that ritual if it meant I could have the snuggly blanket feeling again. That night, when children should have been soundly dreaming of puppies and birthday parties, a fire was ignited in me, a blaze that would continue to burn for many years.

I continued to sneak into my dad's bar on occasion, or find my friend's parent's liquor cabinet if I was at a sleepover. It also didn't take me long to learn that the whole experience could be pleasant from start to finish – and I was a lot less likely to get caught – with a much smaller amount of alcohol. Little did I know that I was starting to form strategies to deceive and manipulate, strategies that would continue to become more sophisticated and elaborate as I got older.

DIDN'T D.A.R.E. TEACH YOU ANYTHING?

By the age of 11, I was stealing cans of beer and taking them to school with me in my backpack. I sought out the girls in my class who had the wildest streaks in them and we would often share the beers in the ladies' room during class breaks. That year, I was in 6th grade, and our school engaged with the city police department to bring in a program called D.A.R.E. (Drug and Alcohol Resistance Education). The purpose of the program was for the police to educate and scare the students about the dangers of alcohol and drugs. They went into great detail about alcohol, illicit drugs, violence, gangs, prison, and the number of injuries and deaths from things like traffic and other accidents, overdoses, and suicide. The intent was to paint such a grim picture that we would be motivated to make healthy decisions when confronted with opportunities to drink or experiment with street drugs.

That didn't work. All the cops succeeded in doing for me was promote additional options beyond alcohol, what those options were called, and what effect they would have. D.A.R.E. opened a door that I didn't know existed and I couldn't wait to run through it.

Alcohol was great and I loved it. I had been drinking periodically for four years by that point, but it was also hard to obtain. I couldn't sneak enough from my home to set off any alarm bells, same with friend's houses – staying below the radar was critical. Eleven was entirely too young for a fake ID and not many people over the age of 21 were keen to buy or provide booze for a kid. So, that was it – time to start researching my next play. One of the most astonishing things about addiction is the mental obsession and the amount of time and exertion that is spent on thinking about the action. That is true no matter how the addiction manifests itself; the action only accounts for a sliver of the big picture. The mental energy that goes into the masterminding and preparing, contingency planning, and evaluating the action could power a small city. My mental obsession was starting to generate intensity and I was unaware that a portion of my life focus was getting caught in a riptide.

A few weeks after our D.A.R.E assembly, I got caught by a Teacher's Aide with a can of beer in the ladies' room. Even though I managed to talk my way out of it, I couldn't prevent the little rumor that spread about the incident afterward. My friend Sarah, probably the most honest and strait-laced student in our class, came marching up to me and blurted incredulously, "Didn't D.A.R.E. teach you *anything*?" I don't think I said anything other than a mumbled apology. I'd never seen Sarah that confounded before. It jolted me. But my internal sly thoughts quipped, "Yeah, actually D.A.R.E. taught me a lot!"

It wasn't until the next year when I entered Junior High School (7th and 8th grades) that I found the "druggies" and started to befriend them. These weren't kids that I felt proud to be seen with and we had little shared interests, but they had the stuff I wanted and I decided that was more valuable than actual friendships. My new social circle introduced me to cigarettes and marijuana and showed me the ropes, plus they always had a considerable supply of alcohol to share as a couple of the guys enjoyed stealing bottles from liquor stores. This was the time, the start of Junior High, when my behavior started to appear noticeably problematic.

Up to the end of 6th grade, I was enrolled in a special Elementary School program for exceptionally bright children, called G.A.T.E. (Gifted and Talented Education). The hand-selected "G.A.T.E. kids" were bussed every morning from several local public schools to the school that hosted the G.A.T.E. program. This small group of students were largely kept together in our designated G.A.T.E. bubble and our interactions were mostly with each other. Just about all of us were good, smart kids who displayed model behavior and exemplary study habits. Even though I had the early signs of addiction brewing, my behavior was still complementary to the other kids I spent time with. Once I graduated from G.A.T.E. and entered my local public Junior High, I became more vulnerable to the behavior of my new "friends" and things started to unravel.

Cutting classes became routine as I favored hanging out in the alleys behind the school campus with my circle, smoking cigarettes and drinking. My grades slipped as assignments were turned in late or not at all and I found myself frequently in the principal's office and being graced with after-school detention for truancy. My friends introduced me to heavy metal (which is still hands-down my favorite genre of music) and I developed a fabricated "I don't give a fuck" attitude. Think: Judd Nelson's character in *The Breakfast Club*. That behavior didn't come naturally and I was starting to experience some serious value conflicts internally. I didn't wear the costume of the bad girl comfortably. But I felt that rebellious behavior was expected to fit in with my new friends and getting into trouble and failing classes was applauded. While I succeeded in gaining the approval I desperately wanted, my sense of self-worth took a big dive. The more I denied my integrity and core values, the deeper I slipped into a well of desperation and confusion. I faltered in developing my own identity in those critical early-teen years because I prioritized two things: 1) feeding my expanding addiction, and 2) securing validation and admiration from those who supplied the ingredients. I was willing to go to extraordinary lengths to achieve that.

I was earmarked at a very young age as a "high potential," a classification that I agree was appropriate. Experts know how to identify strengths and characteristics that are likely to help an individual shine in their chosen pursuit. The road I chose to travel down was probably not what those experts had in mind, but nonetheless, I did not disappoint with my ability to excel at whatever I put my mind to doing. I showed a lot of promise as a budding addict and would continue to hone my craft and become a master in the art of deception.

THE POWDERS

It was in 8th grade, when I was 13, where I expanded my horizons beyond marijuana and alcohol. Introducing: the powders. During 7th grade, while I was exploring my recalcitrant competencies with the suicide squad, my parents' marriage disintegrated and they physically separated. My mom and I moved to a neighboring city and I was thrust into a new school and environment. Perhaps my parents also thought in vain that the move would be good for me to get a fresh start as they were finding my conduct increasingly unmanageable. That hope is usually exhausting and ineffective though, as I would later learn many times over. You can change your physical location as often as you like, but all your unwanted crap will always move with you. I quickly found my chosen people at my new school. They're not hard to spot – they're the ones wearing all black, with heavy makeup, and giving the middle finger to anyone who passes by. By this point, I was fairly experienced with the desired behaviors of renegades and fit in nicely.

At 13, I was also becoming acutely aware of my sexuality and discovering how flirtation and charm could be used for power and manipulation. Oh boy, that was a minefield of tantalizing fun. Teenage boys are easy targets anyway, enslaved by their own delicate hormonal balance. Enter a guileful female with an agenda and it's an unfair match. The girl will win every time. A few of us 8th grade girls were getting bored with the boys in our class. We considered them still quite immature and they didn't have a lot of drugs to offer, so we started hanging around the high school, looking for bigger fish to hook, which required zero effort. One of my friends, Lacie, who was also 13, had a body that was developed far beyond her years and enjoyed flashing her double D's without warning to anyone who was in the vicinity. I felt sorry for the males when she would do that, watching them become flustered and unstable.

Thanks to Lacie's boobs, we befriended a couple of 16-year-old boys and we thought these guys were perfect: reckless, perilous – and they had good drugs. They invited us to parties every weekend and introduced us to cocaine and methamphetamine. Cocaine never grabbed me. I tried it many times and failed to see what the appeal was. Granted, I would never turn it down if it was offered to me, but my response was indifferent. Meth, or speed, was a completely different story. That drug had an effect on me like a firework. It was alarming how much I liked speed immediately. It made me feel superhuman and invincible. I could handle my liquor much better (or so I thought – in truth, it probably just prevented me from passing out), I had a bucketload of energy and everything was sharp, clear, and made sense. Suddenly, I had a new top priority. Get. More. Of. That.

Becoming a meth drug seeker was a whole other level and I was dipping my toe into some pretty dangerous territory. This was not child's play anymore. Sure, underage drinking and marijuana possession carried some hefty ramifications at that time, but that was still considered "soft drug use." If you were caught, you could wiggle your way out of it or get the penalty watered down without too much effort. Not so with the powders. The consequences were much harsher and the number of shady hands those powders pass through before they get to you, the end user, was not a recipe for trust. Plus, the cost factor was a huge obstacle for a 13-year-old. Nonetheless, I have never met another alcoholic or addict that wasn't a master at creative problem solving. If I had applied a fraction of the prowess and energy to other areas of my life that I channeled into drug seeking, I marvel at what I would have been able to accomplish. I got to work on brainstorming crafty solutions.

At this point my drug and alcohol usage was still casual due to the limited resources I was able to obtain, but I found it harder and harder to conceal the noticeable effects of the drug use – especially meth. That shit is hard to hide. Foremost, it made me angry. Really angry. For the couple of years before I got turned on to speed, I was already doing a pretty good job at developing a negative attitude, but with methamphetamine, I cranked up the volume and became plain hateful. I don't really know what I was hateful about: I was not disadvantaged in life in any way, but the drugs messed with my ability to see anything with a clear perspective. I rode severe emotional waves that were exacerbated far beyond what is expected during the teenage years. I developed a habit of snorting a couple of lines of speed daily before school and then spent the six or so hours that I was attending campus with a clenched jaw and perceptible agitation. To make matters worse, speed killed my appetite and my weight dropped. I have a small frame naturally, so a few pounds of weight loss were noticeable – even with baggy clothes. Teachers and school counselors raised the red flag with my parents that they suspected I was using drugs and the confrontations that ensued were ugly. The more the adults in my life tried to push their authority on me, the harder I pushed back. My vigilant defiance raged and I acted out regularly. I screamed and cursed a lot, snuck out of the house late at night, defied any request or rule, and was generally spiteful and bitter. Teenagers are unquestionably hard work. But a teenager on drugs… there is a special place in heaven reserved for those parents.

The thing about any kind of drug, including pharmaceutical medications, is that you cannot pick and choose the effect it will have on you. Drugs are package deals that include unpleasant side effects and it is up to you to examine the contents in that package and decide if it's worth buying the deal. You cannot smoke cigarettes without offensive odors and discoloration to your mouth, teeth, and fingers. You cannot choose the fuzzy blanket or increased confidence feeling from alcohol without the hangover or the depressant effects. You cannot opt in for the increased libido from something but say no thanks to the dry mouth – sorry. With meth, I loved – really loved – the increased energy and the appetite control. In fact, if the only effects of speed were to keep you thin with lots of energy, it would be a desirable drug for most women, and a lot of men. But speed has a sinister side and the more I sold my soul to methamphetamine the more the darkness enveloped me.

I know my parents were trying to help me, and help themselves, too. But they were at a complete loss as to how to manage my out-of-control behavior. I have two older sisters who are both more than a decade older than me and by the time I was seven, both of my sisters had left home. I spent most of my formative years alone in our spacious house, with just my mom and dad – whose marriage was all but formally over. Their physical separation did not last long. My father was diagnosed with cancer a few months after my mom and I moved out and she, probably feeling a mix of obligation and guilt, moved us back into our family home where my parents took up residence in separate bedrooms.

Because of all the turmoil my parents were experiencing, they often got so caught up in their focus on each other that I went unnoticed or was ignored a lot. And when they tried to reign me in, it was futile. I rebelled in so many ways that they ran out of energy to try to punish me. I would do the opposite of what they told me to do, so they gave up on me and took it out on each other, blaming each other for my failures. It was distressing for me to hear the words they used, as I internalized all of the venom that was spat with the words. I didn't understand what "limiting beliefs" were until I was in my 30s, but it was in these years that a lot of my limiting beliefs were formed.

A limiting belief is something that you believe to be true that limits you in some way and is often formed in your younger, impressionable years or by significant life experiences. These beliefs often prevent you from seeing your own strengths and keep you stuck by focusing on the negative elements of your circumstances or how you perceive yourself to be.

Both of my parents disagreed with the other's parenting style and ideas on how to tame my behavior. But of course, I couldn't differentiate that the core problem was about them and not about me. What I heard were things like, "Nikki just wants you to praise her!" and then "Nikki isn't achieving anything worth praising!"

The truth was, I really wasn't doing anything praise-worthy. I was flunking out of school, and thanks to my G.A.T.E. reputation in my shadow, I couldn't pretend that I wasn't capable of being a top student. I was also spending all of my free time with known drug users and didn't get involved with any social activities or sports. So no, I was not achieving anything worth praising at that time. But, when you hear those words come out of your parent's mouth, they sting your soul and attack your self-confidence like flesh-eating bacteria. I still struggle to this day with the words achieve and worth. Achieve = Worth. I must achieve to be worthy. Even when you identify and change limiting beliefs, they never completely go away. They linger. But when you acknowledge their existence, you gain control and can make conscious choices over whether to listen to them or not. I still hear the ghosts of many limiting beliefs rattling around in my head every day, but I have learned how to diffuse their power.

I can still access the shame I felt when I think back about the way I behaved at that time, especially towards my family. I certainly wasn't acting congruent with my core values, not that I had any clue what my core values were then. Metaphorically, I describe it like I was wearing someone else's wet bathing suit – I just didn't feel right in my own skin. I felt trapped. I couldn't articulate a feeling like disgrace or remorse, but I certainly felt it. If you can't describe a feeling, you can't understand it. If you can't understand it, you surely can't manage it. In the absence of any kind of control over my emotions, I sank deeper into my introverted and tormented soul. The further down I went into my emotional grave, the more desperate I became to numb myself with any substance I could get my hands on.

DEATH BY A THOUSAND CUTS

Cutting. It's a practice that is common and widely misunderstood. It can understandably look like a suicide attempt to someone who is unfamiliar with cutting, but it is not. Cutting is a form of self-injury by making small cuts on the body, usually on the arms or legs. It is often, but not exclusively, practiced by early-teens to teenagers as a way of releasing emotional pain. Kidshealth.org explains it like this:

> *"People who cut may not have developed positive ways to cope.*
> *Or their coping skills may be overpowered by emotions that*
> *are too intense. When emotions don't get expressed in a healthy*
> *way, tension can build up – sometimes to a point where it*
> *seems almost unbearable. Cutting may be an attempt to relieve*
> *that extreme tension. For some, it seems like a way of feeling in*
> *control."*[1]

I started cutting my first year of High School in 1991. Because of the temporary move with my mom in 8th grade, I was now in my third new school in three years and I was really struggling with the social aspects of adolescence. I didn't feel like I belonged to any group. My addiction was completely in the driver's seat, but I no longer wanted to hang out exclusively with the derelicts. We had no common interests beyond using and I was starting to feel like that wasn't enough for me... but I didn't know what I wanted or where I fit in. I struggled with my identity and what my interests were and started to realize that my behaviors the previous few years had stunted me emotionally and socially.

High School, from my experience of American high schools in the 80s and 90s, is notoriously social. This has been correctly evidenced by Hollywood movies of the 80s like *Pretty in Pink*, *Fast Times at*

Ridgemont High, and *Ferris Bueller's Day Off.* I wanted my high school experience to be full of teenage angst, first loves, and football games. Essentially, what I wanted was the best of both worlds: a steady supply of meth and alcohol supplied to me by my addiction-encouraging "friends" but spend my time with the "cool kids." Naturally, that delusion left me out in the cold and increasingly isolated from all social circles. I wasn't authentic with anyone and people could easily perceive that. Cutting became a way for me to manage the emotional pain and confusion I was feeling. It seems like it shouldn't make sense for physical pain to be a reliever for emotional pain, but it is. Self-injury can release endorphins that mimic the high you get from cocaine or speed and it becomes a source of comfort. The blood that flows is also symbolic of the emotional pain leaving your body.

I had a stash of straight razor blades that I used to "chop lines" with (finely cutting powdered drugs to break down any clumps or rocks prior to inhalation), and one of them became my designated cutting blade. I chose places on my body that were easy to access and hide – forearms and thighs mostly. I didn't get caught doing this for many months until my eldest sister was visiting home one weekend and she noticed diagonal scabs – like a cat had swiped me – on my forearm immediately. She asked me what happened (we didn't have a cat) and I told her that I had been pruning the rose bushes in the garden. She gave me a doubtful look, but didn't say anything further. Inside, I was screaming, "Please help me!" but my facial expression was closed and didn't invite any further discussion.

This was one of the first times I remember so clearly that I wanted to bawl and plead for help, but the words stayed stuck in my hollow chest. I was nearing a breaking point; I was 14 years old and I had been drinking and using drugs for half my life. I couldn't handle the crushing weight of lies and secrecy anymore. The highs weren't worth it. The pain was too much to bear. I couldn't speak. My silent pleas remained hostage inside my soul.

I still have some of those cutting scars on my forearm. Most of them have faded, but a few remain as a reminder of my anguished younger self. I look at them now with sadness and my heart aches for that little girl who was so desperately lost.

RAT POISON

Funding my drug habit was proving to be quite the obstacle, even though at 14, I now had my first job working after school and on weekends. I couldn't spend a large amount of my earnings on drugs because I wouldn't be able to hide that from my parents, but a small portion was channeled into bags of meth regularly. However, I had another problem surfacing: tolerance. As my body was getting used to regular doses of speed, the same amounts weren't having anywhere near the effect that they previously did. I had to keep upping my quantities which meant that my stock ran low quickly. I needed more money. I really didn't want to dip my toe in the world of dealing because then you are seriously asking for problems with the law. But, some of the guys in my circle dealt and they fully supported their own habit that way, with cash to spare.

I weighed up the risk and reward of becoming a small-time dealer and ultimately decided that the idea made sense. I learned some tricks and started casually dealing meth to other people at my school and neighboring schools. Yes, it solved the money issue for a while, but I was extremely uncomfortable doing it. Just using meth alone causes paranoia and delusions, but the dealing added so much more complexity about getting caught, going to jail, or even getting killed. I didn't want to do it. I didn't want to get sucked into that world of violent crime. I was a nice, smart, pretty girl from an upper-middle class family. I wasn't a criminal. All I wanted to do was support my own habit. I decided to maximize the stash I had left, sell it all, and then stop dealing altogether.

The truth about any street drug is that you never actually know what's in it or where it came from, but you can pretty much count on one thing: it's not pure. There is no Walter White out there selling crystal meth that is 100% chemically uncontaminated. Usually, the more hands the drug passes through, the more "fillers" are put into it. Drug users are aware of this and it's a big gamble to trust the product you are sold enough to put it in your body. Meth also tastes awful so the additives that speed is often "cut" with tend to have a pungent taste to blend well. Some of the more common additives that you see in speed are: lithium metal, caffeine tablets, cold and flu products, hydrochloric acid, iodine, sulfuric acid, and red phosphorus.[2]

I typically used caffeine tablets to cut my supplies before reselling because they were bitter, easily blended, and were relatively harmless. But one time, I didn't have any caffeine tablets and so I went looking around the house for creative powders I could use. I ended up out in the backyard shed and saw a large jar of rat poison. *Don't even think about it, Nikki,* the voice in my head warned. Out of curiosity I stepped nearer to the jar, with the voice in my head getting more forceful. Another voice spoke up, *What if I just used a little bit...? It is the right color and has an odor that would be passable...* My conscience was on high alert now. *This is not a good idea. Do not mix rat poison into the bags you are about to sell.* The voices of warning in my head seemed to multiply, like they had attracted a crowd of onlookers and now the emergency lights and sirens were going crazy. *You could really hurt someone, maybe even kill them. STOP! What are you doing? What are you DOING!*

Then, the strangest thing happened. My body switched into a depersonalized state and I felt like I was watching the scene from above my body. My arms moved toward the lid of the jar, I reached in and extracted a few pellets and put them in my pocket, I closed the lid, and walked away trembling. I did not feel in control of those physical movements. It was like someone else was operating the control panel in my brain.

I methodically cut the pellets into the mix and portioned out the bags. Then, I numbly sat on the floor for what seemed like hours before pouring the whole batch down the toilet. I couldn't bring myself to go through with selling it, but the damage to my self-respect was done. I hated myself for even *contemplating* using poison in the first place as an additive to a drug that was already so detestable. But then, the *action* of actually cutting the pellets into the mix was so heinous that there was no justification for it and no way to blame anyone else. I felt hollower than I had ever felt before. I couldn't look at myself in the mirror after that. I withdrew from all my friends and activities – anything that brought me joy. I didn't deserve it. I was smart enough to know that you should never, ever trust a drug dealer. I had just observed that I couldn't trust myself either. I wasn't better than the derelicts I placed myself on a smug pedestal above. I was just as despicable.

My breaking point had finally come. My self-worth had finally lost her last petal and there was nothing more to do but wither up and die. I needed to get help. I sucked up my pride and my last shreds of human decency and asked my parents to help get me into a treatment center.

ALCOHOLICS ANONYMOUS

Soon after, I was admitted into a 30-day inpatient youth rehabilitation facility that was a dedicated wing of a hospital called Positive Action Center (PAC). It wasn't a bad place to be. The staff were really kind and supportive and the counsellors were mostly former alcoholics and addicts themselves, so they "got it." It was the first time I had really felt understood and I could speak honestly about my actions and my feelings without worrying that I was either going to scare the person I was speaking to or be looked at with disgust.

There was one counsellor in particular, Wayne, who made a lasting impression on me. Wayne was a loud, long-haired hippie in his mid-30s who wore patchouli oil and had a no-bullshit attitude. He hurt my feelings a lot because he was blunt, but once my ego got over it, he earned my respect. He was honest and humble about his past and appeared like he carried no lasting shame. That intrigued me because all I felt was disgrace and remorse.

Still today, we (society, the world) have a long way to go in our perceptions of addiction – or any mental health condition, really. But it's a lot more acceptable to talk about it now than it was in 1992. Wayne gave me a sense of hope and relief, maybe for the first time ever, that I was not a bad person. I had a disease called addiction and having that disease is not a matter of will. Your choices are fully in your control, but being born with the DNA that carries an addictive gene is not something that anyone selects for themselves. This knowledge empowered me and made me feel like I had a second chance ahead of me. I wanted to be like Wayne. Maybe less of an asshole, but I wanted his vigor and enthusiasm, and his ability to accept himself fully, regardless of what other people thought of him.

PAC also gave me my first introduction to Alcoholics Anonymous (AA). The hospital kept you in a protective bubble for the first ten days of your stay, allowing your body to fully detox anything that might be in your system with nurses monitoring you around the clock. But once you were medically cleared you were allowed some interaction with the outside world: namely, family visits and AA meetings at night. Some of the AA meetings were onsite and others the PAC patients were driven to so I got to know a good mix of people and meeting formats. It was wonderful and I discovered that there were a lot of "Waynes."

Being introduced to AA is unequivocally one of the best things that has ever happened to me. AA has saved my life countless times. No matter how many times I stubbornly denied my addiction and swore that "this time" would be different, only to come stumbling back, broken and defeated with my tail between my legs, the members of AA always welcomed me back with open accepting arms and no questions or judgment – just a hug and an "I'm glad you're here." The rooms of AA meetings are the warmest and safest places in the whole world. They're like freshly baked bread for your emotions.

After my 30-day stay at PAC and my return to the "real world," the next three years were some of the best years of my whole life. I had to make some tough decisions that my family didn't always endorse, like choosing to leave high school and finishing my high school education as an independent student. This scared my father as he viewed it as "dropping out" of high school. In his mind, getting a university degree was compulsory and I was breaking the path that would lead me there. I didn't feel that I could stay in my traditional high school and try to blend in with all the other students. I had been through too much, was thriving in my sobriety, and didn't want to reopen the door to my past by trying to resume the same conditions that I had previously been in. Life hadn't just pressed the pause button for me. I had changed. I couldn't risk going backward.

My mother fully supported the decision to take on independent study and the divide in my parents' viewpoints didn't make our home life any more comfortable. It drove the wedge between them even farther and the arguments with me as the subject became more frequent. Those limiting beliefs that I was bad, didn't deserve praise, and that I wasn't achieving anything worthwhile loomed mightily in my psyche. I felt like nothing I did earned my father's love and that I was just a disappointment to him. He was a proud man who was a self-made success story and had strong beliefs about hard work and discipline. He did not agree with or support shortcuts in any way, nor was he receptive to other perspectives. My mother was becoming increasingly codependent. Perhaps it was her way of wanting to protect her young by padding all the walls so life couldn't break me again, or maybe it was a way to satisfy her resentments against my dad, or probably a bit of both. Whatever either of their motives were, neither were wrong, just irreconcilable. Sides were taken in my family and my mother's side was the more pleasant one for me to choose. My dad was thrust out of the decisions when it came to my teenage development and it fractured the relationship I had with him even more. With my mom's support in everything I did, he became perceived as the obstructor and the enemy. It took another 20 years for those wounds between my dad and I to heal.

In my independent studies, I flew through all my high school equivalency requirements. My intelligence, once unclouded by my drug-induced haze, shone once again. It took me a total of 18 months to complete four years of classroom instruction and exams and I entered a community college at 15 years old to begin my associate degree – a two-year degree that would allow me to enter a university as a Junior and complete the last two to three years of a bachelor's degree at that institution. I was determined to prove my father wrong: I would attain a university education, but I was going to do it my way.

I developed strong friendships with people from AA and had a flourishing social life. Because of its anonymous nature, the AA community was like an underground metropolis. Unless you were aware of the strength of the network, you would be oblivious of its enormity. I had friends from every walk of life – CEOs, ex-cons, (CEOs that were also ex-cons), nuns, politicians, mothers, teachers, lawyers, teenagers, bikers, entertainers, doctors – it was a melting pot of personalities and life experiences with one thing in common: we were all recovering alcoholics and addicts with a desire to stay sober. And the meetings were fun. Oh boy, did we have fun. Most of us had rediscovered what we once lost, our zest for life, so we did a lot of making up for lost time in those rooms. Life was fantastic. I was happy and progressing and all was right in my world… until addiction reared its ugly head again, this time in a different form.

PAT AND KRISTIN

Eating disorders suck. No matter how you attempt to define or measure it, eating disorders are hard to treat because there is so much grey area. With illicit drug abuse, it's pretty black and white – you either use or you don't. Alcohol and prescription drug abuse is a little less clear because it's open to interpretation of what constitutes misuse, but the generally accepted treatment is much easier for alcohol and drugs: abstinence. You can't abstain with food, so the waters are murky when it comes to accurately diagnosing an eating disorder and the effective treatment options for it.

It wasn't a surprise that my disease of addiction would manifest itself as an eating disorder around this time of my life, between 15-18 years old. Teenagers have it tough anyway and body image distortions have become increasingly problematic. According to the National Eating Disorder Collaboration: "studies show that people with eating disorders experience higher rates of other mental disorders, with reports of up to 97% having a comorbid (two or more disorders occurring in the same person) condition. The most common of these are depression and anxiety disorders, followed by substance abuse and personality disorders."[3]

With statistics that high, a snowball in hell had a better chance of getting through my teenage years without food issues than I did. I visualize the underlying disease of addiction like a boiling pot on a stove. If the lid is on tight, without any release valve for the steam to come out, the contents will eventually boil over and there's a high probability that it will be forceful and messy. If the lid has open vents or is placed slightly askew, there's more room for the steam pressure to release, but some of the contents might still come up to the surface and possibly spill a bit.

A sober addict or alcoholic can get complacent in their recovery, feeling like they've never had it so good – a condition often referred to as being on a "pink cloud." They can cease or substantially slow down doing the recommended improvement work on themselves and might stop attending AA meetings altogether because they convince themselves that they were just going through a "rough time" and now they're fine. The improvement work and the meetings are like steam valves, and without those healthy releases, this individual is likely to relapse – and that can certainly be forceful and messy.

Then, there are those who follow a suggested program of recovery, engage with their support network, and do the work on themselves

– so they have all sorts of valuable releases actively in use. The disease can still surface like the contents in the boiling pot and leak out a bit, it just doesn't make as big of a mess. This was my experience with disordered eating. In those years between 15-18, I remained sober and active in my recovery, but I engaged in both anorexic and bulimic behaviors as a way of calming and managing the undercurrent of anxiety I felt and the painful emotions and memories that still haunted me.

After about two years of practicing disordered eating, my weight had dropped to the point where I was medically underweight. Not severely underweight, but enough to provoke my mother to take me to see an eating disorder specialist. I don't remember the lady's name, but I remember that she had a soft, feminine demeanor and her office was excessively pink. Her clothing even matched the decor with cashmere and lace sweaters. The whole suite looked like a wedding cake. She was a far cry from Wayne. I only saw her a handful of times, but they turned out to be incredibly potent sessions because she taught me about the power of labelling and visualization.

First, she asked me about how I felt about myself when I was engaged in, or wanted to engage in, destructive eating behaviors (either skipping multiple meals or a binge/purge cycle). I described the feelings and she coached me to visualize a person in my mind who represented who I was when I was in those behaviors and give them a name. That was Pat. (Note to anyone reading this whose name is Pat: This is not you. You are beautiful.)

The "Pat" that I visualized was as nondescript of a human being as she could possibly be. If you saw her in public, you'd likely spend a minute or two pondering if she was a man or a woman and not feel convinced about your conclusion, if you came to one at all. She had a short body with a barrel chest, no apparent breasts or waistline, fat fingers, and a dirty brown mullet. She wore brown pants with a checkered shirt that had food stains on it and was tucked into her pants sloppily, a white undershirt, and scuffed brown shoes. She had a noticeable moustache on her upper-lip, brown nicotine stains on her crooked front teeth, and two crusty moles on her chin and cheek with long grey hairs poking out of each mole. Her voice was loud and gruff, she spat when she talked, and her vernacular sounded dreadfully uneducated.

Then, the cashmere lady asked me to visualize who I was when I was in my healthiest, happiest, and most charismatic behaviors and to name that person. That was Kristin. Kristin was stunning and graceful. She was tall and slender, with noticeable lean muscle definition, and a healthy golden tan. She wore a crisp white fitted pantsuit with a cobalt blue silk shell under her jacket and nude heels. Her jewelry was simple with diamond studs in her ears and a diamond and white gold necklace to match. She had long, thick wavy blonde hair, straight white teeth, and dimples in both her cheeks when she smiled. Her turquoise eyes sparkled and held such kindness. Her voice sounded like a Disney princess and her tone emitted confidence and calm. You couldn't help but light up when Kristin was near you; she radiated positivity and goodness. You felt loved and invigorated when you were with Kristin.

The cashmere lady didn't speak at all as I was describing these two characters in vivid detail with my eyes closed, but I heard her pen scribbling notes. After I was done and opened my eyes neither of us spoke for a long pause. She finally broke the silence and observed, "There's a lot of Christ in the name Kristin." I hadn't consciously thought of it that way, but the connection was certainly there. I had visualized a person who was pure and made me feel comforted and that person was who I saw when I was at my best.

I still frequently use that particular technique of visualization myself, as well as with clients who I coach. Sometimes it's a person that is visualized, given a name, and associated with a particular situation or behavior – like Pat or Kristin. Sometimes it's an object, like a cassette tape or vehicle, that aids to visually understand and manage a process. Pat and Kristin are still two of my star players. I awaken them frequently, but not in relation to destructive eating patterns. They represent feelings, fears, limiting beliefs, and abundant self-love. By inviting them to the forefront of my mind, I give myself the power to make conscious choices about who I allow to be in charge. Pat is guided by fear and is predominantly pessimistic, but sometimes she has legitimate concerns, so I show her respect by listening to her voice those apprehensions. Sometimes she's full of shit, too, so I thank her for her contribution and then ask her to quietly take her place in the backseat. Kristin is trustworthy, uplifting, optimistic, and has gravitas. She does most of the driving.

Why is visualization so powerful and effective?

Visualization harnesses the power of our subconscious mind so that we can make sense of, gain control of, and reprogram the thoughts, emotions, and patterns that are humming in our mind but that we aren't always consciously aware of.

Visualization also helps program the Reticular Activating System (RAS) which is a bundle of nerves by our brainstem that acts as a filter for the eight million bits of information that are pinging around in our brains at any given time. The RAS thinks in images, not words. When we attach pictures to bits of information, the RAS can filter the information differently, thus allowing us more conscious control over what we pay attention to. I talk more about visualization and the RAS in Chapter Ten: You Got This (SELF-TALK).

I HAVE NOTHING TO GAIN FROM YOU

Eighteen is the magic number in the US where you are a legal adult and free to make your own choices. At 17, I started to make my mental plans about how I was going to spread my wings beyond Southern California. I had itchy feet. I wanted to travel and see the world and flex my muscles of independence. I was nearly three years sober and starting to be perceived as responsible enough to make big decisions.

I looked at study abroad programs where I could continue my university studies and gain life and language experience overseas. Spanish was my chosen language as I already spoke some Spanish being from a Mexican-American family and nearly 40% of Southern Californians are Spanish speakers. I turned my friend, Heather, who was also sober, on to the idea and we started making plans to take this adventure together. Spain was our country choice and we were accepted to the University of Granada for a six-month immersive language program.

The first couple of months were fantastic. Heather and I got to know the other students in our foreign studies program and we did a lot of sightseeing together as a group. The whole environment, culture, and behavior in Spain was so different from anything I had ever experienced. I had travelled internationally a lot with my family, but this time I was on my own, making my own decisions, and I loved it.

After we settled into the lifestyle, the initial large group that we hung out in started to break off into smaller groups as people discovered more or less common interests in others and became more selective for companionship. Heather went one way and I went another. In the States, we shared so many common interests and spent a lot of time together. In Spain, Heather and I gravitated toward different things that captured our attention. I still saw her daily in classes and around campus, but we weren't hanging out on weekends anymore. She was the only other sober student and, with her, I felt strength. With my new friends, I was the only person not drinking wherever we went.

Most of us foreign students were between 18-21 years old. The legal drinking age in the US is 21 and in Spain it is 18. For many of the students, being able to drink legally for the first time ever was exciting and they wanted to take full advantage of that. Spain also has quite a drinking culture and the Spanish certainly know how to party. Because of the long siesta in the middle of the day, people tended to schedule their evenings much later. Bars often didn't open until 1 or 2 am, and some nightclubs were notorious for not opening their doors until 5 am.

Needless to say, I felt enticed by my new friends' eagerness to drink and wanted to curiously explore this seductive world where clubs kicked off as the sun was rising. My AA community was halfway across the world, Heather wasn't with me to be a positive influence, and I started to engage in the self-talk of: *It probably was just a phase. I mean – you were so young, but now you are much wiser and you know better, three years was a long time to be sober – I'm sure you won't have a problem now.*

I was an absolute pushover for those mental pro-drinking arguments and for the next four months had a blast attending classes during the day, and bar-hopping and clubbing every night. It was exhilarating. I never disclosed anything to Heather about starting to drink again. I resisted being honest with her and justified that I had no obligation to open up because we only saw each other on campus.

Then one day (I don't know how she found out), Heather came marching across the plaza toward me, red-faced with narrowed eyes, and confronted me about relapsing. I admitted it and tried to play it down like I was only having a few sips every once in a while, and it was no big deal. I'm guessing the story she heard wasn't about me having a few "no big deal sips" because she stood there dumbfounded with her mouth hanging open like she couldn't believe what she was hearing. I could feel the last three years of our devoted friendship flashing before her eyes. I froze and held my breath, wondering what she was going to do next. She regained her composure and slowly and evenly whispered, "I have nothing to gain from you." With that, she turned on her heel and walked away. Heather and I never spoke again.

When I look back on my life and recall the countless things that my addiction destroyed, losing Heather's friendship was one of the most devastating. I loved her like a sister and I chose my addiction over her. This was the first important relationship that I lost due to my addiction and my heart wasn't prepared for it. I sank back into my parade of limiting beliefs and negative self-talk and her final words to me echoed in my head. A large dark cloud loomed over Spain for me after that and as much as I tried to shrug it off, I grieved for my friendship with Heather.

DUI

I spent an additional six months backpacking around Europe after my studies concluded in Spain. When I returned to California, I didn't go back to my AA network. After a year overseas, I had successfully convinced myself that what I went through between ages 7-14 was indeed a phase and that I was fine and could manage my drinking now that I was an adult. I was still two years away from being legally allowed to drink in the US, but through some creative resources I secured a fake ID and *voilà*, I was 22 whenever I needed to be.

I worked in sports bars at night and had a full-time class schedule during the day. I had completed my Associate of Arts degree and was now working towards my bachelor's degree. I managed that balance well and felt quite responsible. I was drinking moderately (by my standards) and it wasn't causing any negative consequences. I was getting excellent grades and earned enough to pay my tuition without incurring any student debt. What could possibly go wrong?

One Friday night, I excitedly drove to LAX Airport to pick up my friend, Levi, who was visiting from Miami for the weekend. On our way back to the house that I shared with my mom, I suggested we stop by the bar I worked at for a quick drink. It was a sports bar in a huge entertainment complex and it was pretty impressive inside. I wanted to show it off to my out-of-town guest. We had one drink (actually I had about one-third of the drink because my friend who was bartending was intentionally heavy-handed), and then we left to go home and get a good night's sleep. We had a big day planned the next day.

I saw the parked police car when we exited the complex and walked to where my car was parked. It didn't worry me because I was not intoxicated and I would be extra careful as I drove home. Levi and I got in my car and we pulled out of the complex parking lot. I was exhibiting textbook driving skills and could see the police car in my rearview mirror following me out. About one block later, the red and blue lights began to flash. I reassured Levi that it would be fine, I was not over the legal limit. There were two officers and they asked me to step out of the car for a field sobriety test. In California, at that time, police could not administer a breathalyzer test without performing a field sobriety test first. I stayed calm and executed all commands correctly. One of the cops concluded, "Alright, let's go" but the second cop disagreed. I don't know what his reason was (probably that he'd just watched me walk out of a bar) but he pulled out the breathalyzer machine and had me blow into it. I had given the officer my real driver license at the beginning. My fake ID, while it was passable and usually got me served when accompanied by a dazzling smile, would have been sniffed out by my friends in blue. I was trying to do everything right in this situation. The legal alcohol limit in California is 0.08% and I blew way under that, as I was confident I would. What I had failed to remember was that limit did not apply to persons under the age of 21. The legal limit for an underage drinker was 0.00%. Shit.

I was handcuffed and escorted to the back of the police car, my car was impounded, and poor Levi and his suitcase had to take a taxi to my mom's house at 1 am, ring the doorbell, introduce himself, and explain what had happened. It was not a pleasant night for anyone involved. I spent that night and late into the next day in a cell with four other women – three who had been picked up for prostitution and were incredibly rude and a scrawny sewer rat who was off her head on meth and paced all over the cell ripping up bits of toilet paper for hours on end. It cost me $1,500 to get my car out of impound, I lost my driver license for one year, and my insurance company declared me uninsurable and cancelled not only my policy, but my name off every policy in my family where I was listed as a driver. The consequences from drinking were starting to stack up again.

Over the next few years, I danced on the edge of a metaphorical cliff. I refused to admit that my earlier years had been anything more than a phase and I was not an alcoholic. I hadn't used drugs since I was 14, so I didn't even worry myself with whether I was an addict or not, and I kept my weight right on the border between underweight and the low end of the normal range – where it might have raised an eyebrow of concern, but wasn't severe enough to require medical intervention. Besides, I completed my bachelor's degree, I was working full-time and getting promoted, earning decent money, and I had some solid volunteer experience behind me. I figured if my resume looked good then I was achieving things that were worthy of praise and doing "life" well. I was, by all accounts, stubbornly telling the world that I was in control and to back off. God bless us alcoholics because this is what we do, usually to the exasperated tune of driving everyone around us absolutely crazy.

> *"Most of us have been unwilling to admit we were real alcoholics. No person likes to think he is bodily and mentally different from his fellows. Therefore, it is not surprising that our drinking careers have been characterized by countless vain attempts to prove we could drink like other people. The idea that somehow, someday he will control and enjoy his drinking is the great obsession of every abnormal drinker. The persistence of this illusion is astonishing."*
> **— Big Book of Alcoholics Anonymous**

Today, it's easy to recognize that I never drank like other people. That hindsight is crystal clear. I knew it undoubtedly then, too. However, there is an enormous difference between "knowing" and "admitting," even to yourself. There's an even wider divide between "admitting" and "accepting." You can't shortcut that process either. You have to walk the daunting tightrope between each stage and stop at the checkpoints of despair, humiliation, resistance, bargaining, and anxiety. At this point in my life, I knew intellectually and deep down that I was an alcoholic, but the consequences weren't severe enough for me to move to the admitting stage, so I held on tightly to denial. I hadn't slipped off the edge of the cliff yet. Of course, I valiantly tried many of the usual tricks that an alcoholic performs to convince themselves that they are fine:

1. Get new friends who drink as heavily as you do. If you don't stand out, you don't have a problem.

2. Drink at home before you leave to go out so you already have a buzz and therefore order less, thus the evidence shows that you only had "a few."

3. Drink moderately while you are out and then get tanked as soon as you get home and are alone (and tell yourself it's just a nightcap).

4. Drink small amounts once in a while, like only have one glass of wine with dinner and nurse it, to showcase to others that you are in full control and can moderate whenever you want.

5. Allow yourself to drink only certain things, like only drinking beer or wine and staying away from the "hard stuff."

However, my best trick of all was working in the hospitality industry for eight years. I waited tables, tended bars, and held various management positions in restaurants and nightclubs. Spending 50-60 hours a week in an environment where alcohol is the focus is a fantastic way to persuade yourself that your behavior is normal. There were many places that I worked where I would drink from the start of my shift until the end, but so did everybody else. It was just "the industry."

DR. FEELGOOD

2001 was the year that I plummeted off the side of the cliff. My tango with pharmaceuticals began with a back injury – an alcohol-related injury, of course.

This type of narrative has become entirely too common for many people and it's horrifying:

> *A legitimate injury is treated with strong prescription medication issued by a qualified physician, whom the patient trusts because of their expertise in medicine. Those seemingly harmless and legal tablets prescribed to treat the temporary pain innocently awaken the beast of dependency inside the patient and inevitably sends them spiraling down a long and arduous journey of freeing themselves from the tangled barbed wire of prescription drug addiction.*

On a warm summer evening in July, I was on a date in Laguna Beach. We both had quite a few drinks that night over dinner and we giggled at each other as we made our way back to his car with the elegance of rubber chickens. The concrete path that hugged Main Beach was wet and sandy from the heavy foot traffic of beachgoers during the day. There was a long flight of stairs leading down to a bank of showers where people went to rinse the sand off. As my date and I rounded the top of the staircase and began our descent, my sandal slipped on the wet sand and I went tumbling down the stairs. I was shook up from the fall, but I was so intoxicated that I couldn't articulate where any specific pain was coming from. My whole body throbbed. My date got me home where I climbed into bed and passed out. The next morning, I couldn't walk. I crawled to the bathroom and then called out for my mom to take me to the hospital. I had broken my sacrum and coccyx pretty badly. I had no idea that I had just stepped through the gates of hell, where I would smolder for the next ten years.

The injury had me off work for 18 months and couch-ridden for nine months. The first few months were excruciating. I was slender and didn't have a lot of natural padding on my backside. I couldn't sit so I had to either lay on the couch with the cushions pulled gently apart to give my butt a gap to rest in, or stand up, which was laborious and uncomfortable. Nobody is a good patient when they are confined to a bed or couch for extended periods, but I tend to rate myself high on the restlessness scale in general due to my natural behavior style, so I was not coping well with this arrangement. Anxiety and frustration dominated my days. I was given strong opioids to manage the immobilizing pain and there were no red flags with that because that was considered appropriate treatment for the circumstances. I am quite certain that my treating doctor was unaware that I had a history of addiction; I kept my mouth tightly sealed about that. Perhaps he would have been a tad more cautious if he had known that I was a high-risk patient. Then again, maybe not.

In the late 1990s and early 2000s in the United States, the opioid crisis was just starting to gain traction. Pharmaceutical companies reassured the medical community that patients would not become addicted to prescription opioid pain relievers, and healthcare providers began to prescribe them at greater rates.[4] This subsequently led to widespread diversion and misuse of these medications before it became clear that these medications could indeed be highly addictive, even fatal.[5] Fast forward for reference to 2017, more than 47,000 Americans died as a result of an opioid overdose, including prescription opioids, heroin, and illicitly manufactured fentanyl, a powerful synthetic opioid.[6] That same year, an estimated 1.7 million people in the United States suffered from substance use disorders related to prescription opioid pain relievers.[7] So, 2001 was the most ideal and oblivious time for my disease of addiction to flourish and skyrocket to inconceivable heights.

In those first few months of residency on the couch, my feelings were indeterminate about the narcotics. I approved of the woozy effect they had on me: it was comparable to that snuggly fleece feeling I got from alcohol, but the drugs were also doing their job of reducing the pain, so my focus was less on riding the Care Bear cloud and more on guiding the pain from an 8/10 to a 4/10. Benzodiazepines were eventually added into my rotation to ease the anxiety I was experiencing and keep me calmer, or perhaps that was a gift for my mother who had to deal with my crappy attitude every day.

As my body started to heal and I could resume moderate daily activity, I directed my attention to how I was going to make sure that my prescription supply didn't dry up. Now that the pain was more tolerable, I was able to concentrate on and enjoy the effects of the opioids and I was curious about exploring what else was on the market. The doctor that had treated me since the accident started to make noises about reducing the dosage, so I prepared to terminate him.

I went to a new doctor for an assessment and made up a story that the doctor I had previously seen only treated acute patients and didn't manage chronic pain patients and so I was referred to you (the new doctor). I got a copy of my chart from the original doctor by fabricating some unusual reason why I needed it, so I had records from the accident and the medications that had been used to date. The new doctor got fast praise from me. He gave me a much stronger, longer-acting drug than the one I had previously been prescribed, ideal for managing chronic pain. Marvelous call, doc! You're a keeper. But I didn't stop there.

I continued to shop around at more doctors' offices with a similar tale to tell them. I had little to do on the couch but read, so I educated myself about the nuances of chronic pain and which medications were more potent so I could speak intelligently about the drug options with the doctor. It was extremely manipulative behavior because I was purposely trying to influence the doctor into giving me the strongest medications available by peppering statistics and medical study results about the drugs into our conversation, to the point of sometimes causing the doctor to question their own knowledge or judgment. It worked most of the time. Remember, the drug companies were reassuring doctors that patients would not become addicted to prescription opioid pain relievers around these years. There were some astute doctors who didn't buy into that though and I could sniff them out in the first five minutes of the appointment. If they were more likely to write a referral to physical therapy than a narcotic prescription, I was out of there and they were blacklisted.

I considered doctor shopping and what I could score from them a game – and I was a champion. Every time I went into a doctor's office, the match started and I wasn't leaving until I was victorious. I got into a rhythm of rotating between several doctors who presumed they were my only treating physician – and the only one giving me prescriptions – so I could increase my dosages as I pleased. My tolerance was climbing and I was grossly exceeding the prescribed amounts.

Here I was again teetering on the tightrope between "knowing" and "admitting" and keeping denial securely snug around my shoulders. The evil truth about prescription drugs is that it's effortless to lie to yourself and justify that your behavior is okay, because a doctor prescribed the pills to you. *Doctors are medical experts. They wouldn't prescribe it to me if they didn't agree that I needed it.* That was the story

I was telling myself and I was fiercely sticking to it. I chose to pay attention to that rationalization and turn a conscious blind eye to the other evil truth I knew: that my addiction was raging and there wasn't a doctor in the world who would cosign my behavior if they actually knew the whole story.

Over the following years, my addiction accelerated and I expanded my repertoire of drugs from a range of opioids and benzodiazepines to include barbiturates and amphetamines – and of course, alcohol was always present. I continued to study pharmacology as a hobby and researched the drugs I wanted to experiment with, and usually always obtained them. I had a circle of doctors wrapped around my finger who would welcome me into their office and whip out their prescription pad with a smile. It was as easy as ordering food off a menu and I often felt disheartened that the process wasn't more challenging. I find thrill in the chase. When the gazelle just lays down in front of the lion, what fun is that?

I was also silently living in a state of incessant fear. The amounts and combinations of drugs I was taking were so outrageously high, I knew I was playing with dynamite. I should have become a statistic. I read many stories about famous people who died from prescription drug overdoses and recoiled when I saw the toxicology reports. The pharmaceuticals and amounts that killed them were often far less than what I was swallowing daily. But I didn't have any desire to stop. I was an out-of-control locomotive barreling recklessly down a track to nowhere and I was accelerating so fast that I don't know if I could have found the brakes, even if I wanted to. A crash was inevitable. My pills had become my lifeline and I was prepared to die for them. I was vibrant and full of potential in other areas of my life, but when it came to addiction, I was utterly helpless. The disease of addiction is aptly described as cunning, baffling, and powerful. It steals the soul of its victims and squeezes every bit of life from them in an infinite sadistic ritual, keeping them confused and submissive, succumbing to the master's demands.

My self-respect was annihilated. I tried to display to the world an image of beauty, intelligence, and capability. But I knew it was all smoke and mirrors. I was hungry for external validation and praise to counterbalance the disgust and disappointment I felt inside. I was a fraud, a manipulator, and a liar. I hated myself, really hated myself. I was in so much agony that all I wanted to do when I was alone was heave heavy sobs and plead for it to stop. The only way I could bear to continue functioning was to take more pills to conceal the ache in my cavernous soul.

The real icing on the cake was that I was now severely underweight and my body was going to reach its capacity with the damage I was doing to it at some point. So, if accidental overdose wasn't in my crystal ball, then heart failure probably was. The amphetamines I was taking daily caused my appetite to be constantly suppressed, so food was generally undesirable. But there was a control factor, as well. I was so impotent against the addiction that I became desperate to latch on to anything that gave me an illusion of control. What and how much food I consumed was something that felt manageable. The irony there was that in my desperate bid for government over my food consumption, I was losing even more rule over my physical health and becoming alarmingly emaciated.

Hiding my true weight from anyone was challenging and I was especially concerned about the perceptions of the doctors who were prescribing me amphetamines. The scale was a routine stop that the nurses made between the waiting room and the treatment room and I would stuff my pockets full of rolls of coins or hide my paperweight-laden handbag under my clothing to try and tip the scale downward.

I might have won those battles with the physician's scale, but I eventually lost the war with my family. My mother was especially petrified that she was going to find me dead one morning, Karen Carpenter style. It was just the two of us in our home and she was preoccupied with protecting me despite my vicious attempts to keep her at an emotional distance. To this day, I can't imagine the constant angst she felt. Helplessly watching your child slip away must be one of the most excruciating experiences a parent can endure.

RANCHO PALOS VERDES

I didn't feel that anorexia nervosa was an accurate diagnosis, but I conceded to the eating disorder (ED) specialist's classification. I knew that I was disclosing some truth, but hiding an enormous amount as well, so I couldn't blame their assessment because it was based on what they were aware of. My mother begged me to see an ED specialist, to which I finally agreed because I was emotionally bankrupt and honestly didn't have the energy to fight anymore. The ED doctor was quick to suggest that inpatient treatment was absolutely necessary and my lifespan would be limited if I didn't get help. Okay doc, on that we could agree.

In the initial assessment sessions, I never disclosed anything about prescription drug use. I was extremely protective of that and was not about to put those lifelines that I had worked so hard to create in jeopardy. I admitted to a history of alcoholism and disordered eating in my teens. I couldn't deny that because they were interviewing my family members as well so those skeletons were going to be dragged out whether I liked it or not. I admitted to using illicit drugs in my early teens but correctly asserted that I had not used illegal substances since then. If they had known that I was taking high doses of prescription amphetamines daily, it might have had an influence over the diagnosis, but I was more willing to enter a 60-day inpatient facility to treat anorexia than I was to be fully transparent about my actual behavior.

The residential treatment facility that was chosen was stunning and I hated it immediately. It was a house at the end of a quiet cul-de-sac on a cliff overlooking the ocean in Rancho Palos Verdes, California. The real estate value alone was phenomenal and I suspect a lot of people would have looked at the views and eagerly handed in their freedom for 60 days to chill and absorb that privileged slice of California's exquisite coastline. They allowed a maximum of six patients at a time so the house was cozy and intimate. I don't know if they ever had a male patient venture through but the decor was tastefully feminine. The vibe was soft and delicate and exuded peace and calm. I felt suffocated by it. If there is anything that causes me to feel the least amount of peace and calm it is a day spa-esque environment with a gentle undercurrent.

I perceived a couple of the other patients as weak and childish because they sat around all day hugging their teddy bears and moaning about how much they hated their bodies. I was aware that I was probably overgeneralizing their condition, but I couldn't help those feelings of disdain and the desire to categorize myself differently. I didn't understand why I wanted to put myself on a pedestal of moral superiority at that point, but I have come to learn that "terminal uniqueness" is a ubiquitous condition in addiction.

Terminal uniqueness is a false belief that your experiences with addiction are different to anyone else's. This is often an unconscious way of demonstrating self-protection by convincing yourself that other addicts are unable to relate to you, or self-comfort that you are better than others because you haven't gone down the scale as far as they have. While everyone's experiences with addiction are distinctive, addicts tend to have more things in common than not. Terminal uniqueness causes the individual to dismiss that fact and instead focus on the differences and exaggerate them in their heads. I now believe that terminal uniqueness is not just limited to the disease of addiction, but is common to all human behavior. It is a pattern I frequently see with my coaching clients and in my everyday interactions with people in general.

Maybe it was because I didn't accept that an eating disorder was my primary problem in the first place so I perceived myself differently to the other girls in the house. My belief was that I had a disease called addiction that manifested itself in many ways and disordered eating was just one of them. This terminal uniqueness also led me to behave as if the rules didn't apply to me since I was different. That's the one that got me into trouble.

While packing my belongings at home the day before I was admitted into this facility, I plotted how I was going to sneak pills in with me. I had committed to reside there for 60 days, but I never had any intention to stay clean for the duration. I knew from my time at PAC years before that the absolute first thing the intake nurses do is search every square inch of your body and your luggage. I understood that was common practice in any rehab facility so I was anticipating it in my new swag temporary home. You have to assume that these intake coordinators have seen every clever hiding spot possible and nothing slips past the keeper. So, my challenge was to outwit them. And I did.

I went to a Salvation Army secondhand store and purchased four old cameras that didn't work. Then, I bought a tray of film canisters and removed most of the film from the cases, leaving some intact as decoys. I portioned out the pills I was going to take with me in small plastic bags and then stuffed the bags of pills inside the hollow film case. I then put the film case back inside its plastic container, with the open end on the bottom. This way, if it was inspected you would identify the plastic container as a film canister, open it and see the roll of film. As long as no one took the roll out of the canister and looked at the underside, I would be fine. I memorized where I placed the decoys in the tray to facilitate a demonstration if necessary. In the back of each camera I layered more bags of pills and one film roll stuffed with pills, then closed the cover. By giving the illusion that there was an active roll of film in the camera, I knew that no one would dare to open it.

For the first couple of weeks that worked flawlessly. I was strategic about when I ingested anything, avoiding counselling sessions or group therapy times when a behavior change could be detected, and ensured the amounts I took were low. To fully play the part, every few days I would take one of the cameras out to the backyard and pretend to marvel at the scenery and take stunning photos. I thought I had it nailed. Until I didn't. My roommate came into our room unexpectedly one day when I had the back of a camera open. She saw the multiple bags of pills and ran out of the room. I hurriedly put it all away and jumped on my bed with a book, but roomie and a nurse came in a minute later. The nurse was stern and demanded to have the camera. I tried to play innocent, but she wasn't buying it. Reluctantly, I handed her the camera. She confirmed what was inside and then asked for the other cameras. I knew I was screwed, so I gave her the other three. Then she called another staff member in the room and ordered me and roomie out so they could undertake a full sweep of all my belongings. Needless to say, they called my family soon after and informed them that they would be discharging me that day and to please come pick me up. Everyone was furious, the staff kept all the pills they confiscated (which was all of them), which made ME indignant, and my family were livid and exasperated. I'd let them down once again.

The discharge nurse pulled me aside before I left and, with a smile playing at the corners of her mouth, whispered, "That was brilliant. I have never seen a more creative smuggling of contraband in all my years, and I thought I had seen it all. I hope you put those skills to good use one day."

OXNARD

The tragic truth about treatment centers for any addiction is that they are expensive and scarce. I have seen this to be true in both America and Australia so my interpretation is that it is a widespread theme in other countries as well. Over the years, I have empathetically listened to countless stories of desperate individuals and families who struggled to get help for themselves or their loved one, with some successful and some downright horrifying results. In some cases, families spend years and hundreds of thousands of dollars before they find treatment that works – if they ever do. In my case, my family spent an extraordinary amount of time soliciting guidance from medical experts and insurance companies and speaking to treatment centers nationwide to try to find any available and suitable place to help save my life. After my little stunt in Rancho Palos Verdes, they were more discerning about finding locations that specialized in comprehensive approaches to treat comorbid conditions.

They finally thought they had hit the jackpot when they found a place with availability in Oxnard, California, less than two hours from where we lived. I was largely left out of the decision-making process at that point and ultimatums of "this is the last straw" were being issued towards my behavior.

The hospital in Oxnard was karma's punishment for me fucking up the last place. This center was no ritzy Hollywood dream house: this place had bars on the windows and locked doors. Again, I hated it immediately and now felt resentful that my freedom had been stripped from me. I still wasn't ready to get clean although I was a long way from being able to be honest with myself about that. I went along with the plan and tried to fool myself into willingness. But, oh, the camera trick worked so well the first time. It was my roommate's fault for walking in at the wrong moment (so I told myself); this time I would be more cautious.

I got the cameras by the intake nurses but the plan froze with the director. He explained that due to privacy issues I was not allowed to take any photos inside the facility, and since we were locked in and this was not a beautiful location, I couldn't put up the argument about scenery or landscape photography. I tried the angle of the antiquity of the cameras since they were so old and requested to keep them as decorations in my room. He disallowed that idea, too, as they were heavy and could be used as weapons. I rarely lost a debate, but in this instance, I was defeated. The director promised that he would lock them in a safe in his office and I could have them back when I was discharged. Great. I had 30 days of forced sobriety to look forward to.

Over the next weeks, I did all the required actions in the treatment program and even managed to convince myself that I was getting better. The future was starting to look brighter. My body was getting stronger, my mental fog was lifting, my family was starting to feel relief and hope, and the encouragement I was receiving from all the people who loved me was astounding. I had so many people that wanted to see me get through this and were cheering me on. I felt better than I had in years. I never forgot about the pills that were locked in the director's office, but I thought about them less often as I focused more on all the underlying issues that drove me to the places I had gone. My head swirled with praise and support and everyone was looking forward to me starting a new chapter in my life. Then came discharge day.

On my final day in Oxnard, the spotlight was on me with many warm wishes and cheers of optimism. I was both excited and apprehensive about going home. I really thought I could do it this time, whatever I thought "it" was. Then, the director brought me my cameras and bid me adieu with words of inspiration and fortitude. As soon as he walked out of the room, the sunshine that filled my thoughts quickly disappeared and dark storm clouds rolled in. With my drugs now secretly and securely back in my hands, every bit of willpower that I thought I had acquired over the previous four weeks quickly dissolved. I stood down to the addiction immediately. All I had to do was wait until I was discharged and out of that prison to swallow a handful of pills, but I didn't. *Cunning, baffling, and powerful.* I didn't think I had taken too many but I miscalculated my tolerance due to the previous 30 days of abstinence. The effects of the drug took hold and within a short time the red flags were up and I was caught.

It took the bewildered staff a while to connect all the dots, and I wasn't in any mental state to offer clear assistance, but it was ugly. Again, everyone was furious with me and I was woefully ashamed of myself. Never ask an addict or an alcoholic to explain to you why they do the things they do. They won't be able to tell you. The truth is, we are just as perplexed about our actions as you are. That's the power of the disease. It fully controls and destroys everything in its wake with no apparent logic. I didn't leave Oxnard that day, either. My antics cost me another 14 days in that place for the professionals to try and untangle my true motives, but this time with a dimmer view of my honesty.

HARRY

The next few years were a roller coaster of highs and lows as I would hit bottom, get clean, stay sober for weeks or months and then relapse, only to start the vicious cycle of self-destruction again. My channel to my medical "dealers" was wide open whenever I wanted to access it and I was valiantly trying to live in this fantasy world where I was in full control of everything without giving up my "right" to drink or take addictive medications. The persistence of this illusion is, indeed, astonishing. Then, I met Harry.

I worked for a guy named Ben, who was the co-founder of a biometric authentication company that was way ahead of its time. Ben was okay, but a bit of a creep, so when his business partner from Australia, Harry, suggested I work for him directly instead of Ben, I was more than happy to make the switch. Harry was a loud, fun-loving Aussie who drank an amount that I found appealing. Harry had big business-development ideas that weren't always sound, but he was different and exciting to me at the time. He needed someone to travel with him around the world to pitch his ideas and the company was footing the entire bill. It wasn't a hard sell. Over the next nine months Harry and I travelled between Los Angeles, London, Nice, and Melbourne. It was thrilling at first, a dream job. I was getting paid to travel and co-host dinners and alcohol-fueled business meetings, but the honeymoon phase wore off pretty quickly.

I first noted that something was not stable about Harry in London. He had a hot temper and one day he had an upsetting conversation with a client. He was furious when he hung up the phone and when I tried to console him afterward, he raised his arm to throw the phone at my head. Cellular phones in that day were not small or light. I ducked and he stopped himself, but I heeded the warning.

We continued to travel and work together, but the arrangement was slowly losing appeal and I got increasingly worried about his behavior. I started to see that underneath the boisterous exterior was a man who had severe mental and financial troubles.

Everything came crashing down in Melbourne in January of 2006. It was the first time I'd been to Australia so I didn't feel "at home" in the environment to begin with. Harry had a severe shift in his behavior soon after we got there. He started to act profoundly different to how he had acted in Europe or the States. It was probably because Melbourne was his home and all of his problems were there waiting for him when he arrived. I learned about a domestic violence incident and legal issues that were pending. Harry closed down emotionally and wouldn't speak with me about it, but I learned enough to understand that it was serious, perhaps leading to jail time. I felt alone and isolated and Harry kept telling me to go home, back to California. I stubbornly refused to leave him. Everything inside of me told me that he was probably right, it was time to cut the ties, but I didn't. I wanted to help him and, in all honesty, when someone close to you has problems that are bigger than your own, it's a refreshing escape to shift your focus onto them and ignore your stuff. A few weeks into our time in Melbourne, Harry had what I can only suspect was a psychotic episode.

We were staying in an apartment in Docklands, a residential area on the waterfront adjacent to the Melbourne CBD, characterized by high-rise apartment towers. Harry started experiencing severe insomnia and hallucinations, hushing me when I spoke because he believed the apartment was bugged. Nothing he did made sense and it scared me. I switched into the mode of a full-time caretaker as Harry continued to deteriorate in front of me. I tried to express my concern and share my observations with the other mutual connections we had in Melbourne, but I didn't feel like I was getting a matching level of urgency back. I even stole Harry's Medicare card out of his wallet and contacted hospitals in the area for guidance. I knew how emergency processes worked in the US for mental health conditions like these, so I was looking for similar processes in Australia. The only real guidance I got was that Harry would have to agree to treatment, and he was too far beyond reasonable at that point. Frustrated, I tried once again to rally the support of our acquaintances, to no avail. I don't know if Harry had a history of this behavior and that was why I didn't feel like my panic was reciprocated or if our acquaintances simply preferred a head-in-the-sand approach to mental health issues, but whatever the reason, I will never know. I ran out of time before I could secure any viable solution.

One night in the middle of the night, I woke up startled. I looked out to the sliding glass balcony door and it was ajar. I rushed out to the balcony and saw Harry holding on to the exterior of the glass wall. Holding back my hysteria, I managed to coax him back over the railing. Perhaps his conscience wouldn't allow him to let go with me standing there. He made me swear not to tell anyone. I promised I wouldn't say anything, but I didn't mean it. I would have lied ten different ways to get him to agree that he wouldn't do that again. I had to get him help urgently. I made a pact with myself that the next day I would find some private time and resume my quest with psychiatric emergency assistance. I watched Harry like a hawk into the next morning, but he knew I was watching him, too. Neither of us spoke. I didn't know what to say or do; I had never been in a situation like that before. All I felt I could do was treat him like a small child until I could convince somebody to aid me. But even the best of us can't hold our bladder forever.

I was only away from the living room for two minutes, but that was all he needed. I came out of the bathroom and saw the glass door open. With dread gripping my heart, I ran to the edge and looked down to see Harry lying on the concrete below. My mouth felt like sandpaper and my whole body quaked as I desperately searched for a phone and struggled to dial 000. The panic and terror rose in my throat as I incoherently tried to explain what happened and remember the details of the location. As soon as the dispatcher confirmed the ambulance was on its way, I ran as fast as I could down the fire escape, not willing to take my chances on waiting for the elevator. As I opened the emergency exit door to the terrace where he had landed, I looked up and saw several people on their balconies taking photographs. I still feel disgust when I replay that image in my mind. The first responders arrived about a minute after I got downstairs and I bleakly stood to the side watching as they went through the motions of CPR. When there was no more hope left, I sat numbly on the concrete next to his body going over every detail in my mind about what, if anything, I could have done differently. Finally, the coroner gently told me I had to leave. I had nowhere to go.

I stayed in Melbourne for a short time after that to assist with the police investigation. They quickly ruled out any foul play on my part but asked me not to leave town until after I gave a formal statement. Out of a mix of guilt and sympathy, I wanted to be available to help Harry's family in any way I could, too. Then, I got that call that anyone physically separated from their family dreads: "You need to come home now."

I left Australia with a vow that I would never step foot in that country again.

WE THOUGHT YOU'D GO FIRST

My mother, who was 65, had been diagnosed with a rare and aggressive form of cancer and was scheduled for emergency surgery in a few days. I returned to California a fragmented emotional mess. My family was compassionate about what I had just been through in Australia, but now was the time to put whatever strength I had together to be present for my mom. She was everything to me, and now, she needed me. On the day of the surgery, my two sisters and I gave her all the blessings and positive energy that we could as she was wheeled away to the operating room. The surgery was supposed to have taken hours to complete and the three of us settled in to what should have been a long day in the waiting room. The surgeon came into the waiting room much sooner than we expected and we understood the grim prognosis.

Over the next two months, I dedicated myself to caring for my mother in hospice. We converted our downstairs office into a hospital room for her and had a fantastic staff of nurses around the clock. I was terrified of losing her. She had supported me in everything I had ever done and carried me through countless times when I couldn't care for myself. I owed her so much more than I could ever repay her for and I was guilt-ridden and stricken with grief that she was now leaving me. I held myself together and poured all my energy into trying to demonstrate to her that I would be okay without her. She was justifiably anxious about how I was going to manage my own life when she was gone. Meanwhile, I was simultaneously experiencing the effects of PTSD with distressing flashbacks from Harry's suicide.

The rumblings of inner strength started to emerge during this time with Mom in hospice. I had two breakthroughs occur during those last two months. One was realizing that once she was gone, there was not going to be anyone to fend for me and I needed to rethink my strategy. My father certainly wasn't going to come to my rescue. He had always taken the tough love approach with me and while I knew how much he loved me, it was sink or swim with him. I couldn't come crawling back to his protective shelter every time I messed up in life, like I did with my mom. The other breakthrough I had was how well I handled the block of time in the lead up to her death. I still had a hell of a lot of growing to do, but the anguish of experiencing two back-to-back major life events – witnessing a suicide and losing a parent – was actually filling me with more positive fuel than it was drowning me further. I love the quote often attributed to Eleanor Roosevelt: *"People are like teabags, not worth much until they're put through some hot water."*

Until that year, most of my hardships were either a direct result of my own poor choices or a situation that I was inadvertently in as a result of my poor choices. I started to see myself a bit like Scarlett O'Hara: shedding her spoiled, vain, and manipulative skin and coming into her authentic, passionate, and determined true power. I began to take inventory of my life choices up to that point and gave weight and attention to what I wanted from my future, who I desired to become, and the steps I was going to have to take to get there.

On the day that our mother passed away, one of my sisters and I were with her and holding her hands when she took her final breath. We called our other sister, who lived nearby and came over right away. The hospice nurse walked the three of us through the steps that would happen next and what actions we needed to take. After all the paperwork was completed for the time being, the nurses packed up all the medical supplies, and the coroner removed Mom from the house. We closed the front door and my sisters and I stood in the front entry for several minutes decompressing. None of us spoke as we collectively caught our breath and let everything sink in. Finally, my eldest sister looked at me with her arms folded across her chest and tears in her eyes. In a soft, broken voice she confessed, "We thought you'd go first." We both looked at our other sister who nodded almost imperceptibly in agreement. I pursed my lips regretfully, my eyes full of sorrow and whispered, "So did I."

That was the first time that anyone in my family had told me directly that they thought I would die and it was the first time that I admitted my agreement with that out loud. I was 28 years old. I was lucky to have made it that far. The "cloak of protection" I wore undoubtedly saved my life countless times and is something I will never clearly comprehend. I created a tidal wave of destruction around me and sped through the years without regard for myself or others, but I don't believe it was just luck. There is a reason why my number wasn't called. I don't dwell as much anymore on trying to understand why I'm alive and someone else who did much less damage is not, but I do live every single day now with a tremendous amount of gratitude because of it and take nothing for granted. Every day truly is a gift.

This chapter of my life had to end. I needed to thank all the lessons I had learned along the way and close the door. I had to abandon my stronghold and all the things that kept me small to discover my true power. It was time to look forward, and become.

"And the day came when the risk to remain tight in a bud was more painful than the risk it took to blossom. Life is a process of becoming, a combination of states we have to go through. Where people fail is that they wish to elect a state and remain in it. This is a kind of death. Living never wore one out so much as the effort not to live. Life is truly known only to those who suffer, lose, endure adversity and stumble from defeat to defeat."

— **Anaïs Nin**

CHAPTER TWO

PIERCING THE SKY

LEARNING TO FLY

In the years following my mother's death, there were a lot of changes. The grieving process was hard for me and it also meant that I had to move out of my mom's house as well. It was the first time in my life that I lived completely on my own and had to learn responsibility quickly. I went back to AA and stayed clean some of the time. I still wasn't fully committed to sobriety, even though the story I told myself and everyone else was that I was. Some of it was a facade that I put up to reassure my family that they didn't have to worry about me. Without Mom, our family dynamics had changed. My dad and his wife of ten years at that point were semi-retired and spent a lot of time travelling and golfing all over the world. I was close with my sisters, but they had their own lives to lead and were entirely too busy to dote on me. Mom was the one whose life was immersed in mine. Unbeknownst to her, she helped me stay sick by providing a safe landing for me at all times. Now that she was gone, I had no choice but to learn to fly.

WELCOME TO AUSTRALIA

Just after Harry's death, I met a man who was a friend of Harry's family. I struck up a friendship with him before my abrupt departure back to the States and we kept in contact. This turned into a long-distance relationship over the years following, including a couple of back and forth visits. I ended up marrying him and relocating to Melbourne in early 2009. The country I swore I would never step foot in again had become my new home. Truth be told, moving to Australia probably saved my life because it cut off my free-flowing supply of prescription drugs. If I had kept the ability to trick-or-treat at those doctors' offices, I never would have been able to achieve lasting sobriety and I would have eventually become that statistic. And if my mom hadn't died, I never would have made the choice to move permanently overseas as we were too close. It's ironic how life gives you what you need, not what you want.

I stayed sober initially for my new husband. I viewed my life with him as a chance to start over completely fresh and I was doggedly committed to that. Then, I had a baby. Being a mother was another incentive that helped me to stay clean for a few more years. But I didn't effectively deal with the underlying stressors and emotional triggers that led me to my destructive coping tools in the first place. I learned about resilience and thought I needed to mentally armor up so I could go to battle with life's challenges. What I understand now is that I incorrectly interpreted resilience as the ability to develop a thick skin, but a thick skin doesn't protect you when the problem is in your insides. Eventually my old friend alcohol reared its ugly head again – with all the deceptive, sneaky behavior that came along with it when I drank.

I rolled out the welcome mat for alcohol because that was easy to obtain and Australia has a strong drinking culture. I tried to get my hands on prescription drugs. Believe me, I tried. I was successful at times, but it was never as effortless and lavish as it was in the States – and the menu was limited. Nevertheless, Australia continues to have a considerable problem with prescription drug abuse and has one of the highest levels of opioid utilization globally.[8] But there was a vast difference between Australia circa 2012 and America circa 2000 when it came to accessing potentially addictive prescription drugs. As much as I tried to replicate the medical arrangement that I had in the States, I finally concluded that my meager and infrequent victories weren't worth the effort and resigned my attention to alcohol. I kept my drinking reasonable for the most part, teasing my disease with little slips of excessive consumption from time to time, but since I was living a completely different life to my California stomping ground, I once again convinced myself that I had everything under control.

THE BEST OF TIMES, THE WORST OF TIMES

In 2014, I steered myself onto a path that led to a pivotal turning point. A recruiter friend of mine, who knew of my passion and experience in coaching and development, recommended that I apply to work with a new education company that was gaining rapid traction and popularity. The business provided professional coaching services to people that were either new to or returning to the workforce after a long absence. I was hired as a Professional Development Coach and was quickly promoted into leadership. The program that I led and coached was a beautiful blend of life and career-enhancing skills that was largely based on the principles of emotional intelligence. I felt incredibly grateful to be working in a capacity of helping people make positive life and career choices and aiding with their process of self-discovery. Being an integral part of my clients' growth was extremely rewarding and it lifted my energy and enhanced the quality of my own life in countless ways. In addition, the team I worked with were an amazing group of people who shared the same core values and felt equally inspired by the work they did. Our department leader was by far the best example of emotionally intelligent leadership that I have ever experienced. Every day was bliss. The whole team became excellent friends and it was a wonderfully motivating culture.

The superb part is that you can't help but learn when you teach. When I talk about my past in this book, I focus primarily on the role addiction played, but along my journey I also picked up some immensely valuable professional development skills and education that gave me a good platform of knowledge from which to coach this program. I was able to share some of this knowledge with my clients, but often it was the questions that they asked in response that caused me to pensively consider some of the ways I was managing my own life and the trajectory I was on.

"If you do not change direction,
you may end up where you are heading."
— Lao Tzu

Most of us have nagging thoughts in the back of our mind about things that we should be doing more of, or less of, or ways that we could be more effective in a certain area. Many people become adept at pushing those nagging thoughts to a dark corner where they can't hear them or learn to turn up the volume in another area of their life to drown out the chatter. The art of distraction and avoidance is a great talent of the subconscious.

When my clients and I would engage in a discussion about something like how well they understood their limitations, or how consistent they were with their commitments and actions, it had a ripple effect on me and provoked me to honestly answer those questions for myself.

Through my job, I became increasingly self-aware that there were many things in my own life that I was pushing to those dark corners and I could do one of two things: courageously confront them or wait for the other shoe to drop and take my chances on the impact. I chose a mix of the two options, which is what most people do. Some things I was willing to address and improve and other things I avoided out of cowardice. That's the thing about bravery, it's not a black and white "you're either brave or you're not." Most of us are incredibly courageous... in some ways. The good news is that, like with any skill, bravery can be developed. Whether or not we give ourselves credit for those acts of bravery or choose to focus on our cowardice is deeply individual.

During my time with that company, I made some fantastic life choices and really took note of the ways in which I was personally excelling and developing. I was living in my values and spending my time doing things I was passionate about. I had been living in Australia for several years at that point, and for the first time since making that big move, I was beginning to feel a real clear sense of fulfillment. I was hitting some fantastic career goals, my marriage was great, my son was the light of my life, my friendships were awesome – everything was on the upswing. There was only one thing that I wasn't brave enough to confront: my addiction, which was quietly lurking in the background waiting for the right opportunity to pounce again.

I put a lot of energy into keeping my drinking "normal" and below the radar. However, the behaviors through which the addiction manifests itself are not the problem, they are merely the symptoms. It's pretty easy to keep the symptoms under wraps when life is going well, and even small bumps in the road can be controlled, or easily recovered from. The real measure is how you regulate those symptoms when the shit hits the fan. I was about to fail that test.

The directors of our company made some poor high-level decisions that ultimately sent the whole business into bankruptcy. At its peak, we had over 800 employees, but the decline was quite rapid. In one year, we had hundreds of layoffs. You would leave on a Friday and come in on a Monday and rows of desk spaces would be empty. We lost entire departments at a time. You never knew what was coming next, or when it was coming for you. The company went from a vibrant, pulsing culture to a depressed and vacant wasteland. The vast, once-humming office building turned into an IT graveyard with small clusters of staff busily keeping their head down and clutching their paychecks until their number was finally called.

Our team of 26, with our amazing leader in the driver's seat, was the only fully-intact team still active on the day the business shut its doors for the last time. We survived the storm that claimed hundreds of jobs in one year. While that was certainly something to be proud of, we still lost in the end, and the toll it took on all of us was intense. For a full year, we operated in hyperdrive, desperately trying to provide ongoing value for our clients and save the suite of programs we had worked so hard to create. We held onto hope that the business would find a saving grace, or a Hail Mary, and remained dedicated to our team to the end. Then, in one callous blink of an eye, it was over.

THE PERFECT STORM

In those last months and weeks before my career came to an abrupt halt, my drinking increased dramatically. My stress levels shot through the roof, I experienced severe insomnia, worries about financial security plagued me, and anxiety and panic attacks became frequent. I was not coping effectively, but doing everything I could to hide it and stay resilient.

After the company folded, I didn't have to stay strong anymore and I collapsed into a black hole of booze and depression. Addiction is a progressive illness. Even if there are periods, brief or extended, where control is maintained and the symptoms are kept at bay, the illness will continue developing. This is true even during periods of complete sobriety. One of my friends from AA back in the 90s liked to say, "My disease is doing push-ups in the back of my head." I fully agree with him. I have heard countless tragic tales of men and women who had considerable periods of sobriety, like 30+ years, who resumed drinking and were dead within days. Over any substantial period, we get worse, never better.

This was the point in my life where all of the elements, past and present, culminated in a perfect storm. I had been through three decades of turbulence with my disease and I was exhausted. I didn't have any fight left in me. I had a rough start to life in Australia and things were finally balanced and I was thriving. I couldn't bear any more instability. I was passionate about my job and the people I worked with and fought to save the business in every way I could. I wasn't aware how emotionally invested I was in it either, until it was gone. When it finally ended, it was a cold-hearted split. Along with the other soldiers that fought by my side, I felt discarded and it crushed me.

This is a perfect example of how we can master the art of distraction and avoidance. In hindsight, I could clearly see that I was sinking for quite some time before the shutdown of the business, but I chose to ignore the warning signs. Instead, I developed a laser-focus on trying to control the things I could not (the business) and turned a blind eye to the things that were in my power (my actions, behavior, and my health and wellbeing). This might seem obviously backwards in theory, but it's remarkably common in practice. How often do you see this happen around you, or do it yourself – focus on the circumstance (another person's behavior, the weather, politics, etc.) and not on what you can influence (how you choose to respond to the circumstance)?

For many weeks following my job loss, I stopped caring about everything and let the darkness of self-destruction envelop me. I had no mental strength left and my disease swooped in and took full advantage of that. I just wanted to stay numb, so I did. The volume of alcohol I drank was tremendous and it didn't take long for withdrawal symptoms to set in when I tried to pull back and moderate the amount, or after a period of sleeping. I quickly found that even when I had glimpses of clarity and wanted to stop, I could not. The physical symptoms were too intense to manage. I felt like I had been doused in kerosene and set alight. I was fully consumed and slave to the disease's almighty power.

Then, something happened in a moment that changed my life entirely. A mentor of mine calls it a "kairos" moment. Kairos is an Ancient Greek word that means the right, critical, or opportune moment. It is a moment within a moment, not calculated by chronological or sequential time, where the impact of that moment is immeasurable.

I sat on the edge of my bed after taking a shower. I struggled to do anything: the anxiety and trembling symptoms were so bad, even taking a shower was a colossal task. I couldn't physically function anymore and I was terrified. Alcohol withdrawal symptoms can be extremely distressing and I had never experienced them to this level before. I wanted to cry, but the sobs wouldn't release. I just sat on the bed staring blankly at the wall, bewildered at why I had let it all come to this. I was miserable and the weight of my entire addiction history lay heavily on me. I felt its pressure, and equally, I felt my resistance to surrender. I grieved for my inability to free myself from those chains of bondage. I wanted to weep in sorrow for the last several years where I had been flourishing and now, here I was once again, a disgrace of my own making.

I heard the front door open and my spine stiffened as my husband's footsteps came closer to the bedroom door. He paused in the doorway for a while and I didn't look at him. I couldn't stand to see the look of distress on his face. There was nothing I could say. Eventually, he came over to the bed and sat down next to me. I tried to hide my quivering hands, but I couldn't. He felt the heat and the perspiration radiating off my body as I fixed my eyes to the wall and focused on trying to regulate my breathing. He sighed softly, "I didn't realize it had gotten this bad." I nodded my head vigorously as tears pricked my eyes. He drew a shaky breath and stammered, "One of these days, I'm going to come home and find you dead. But I'll know you didn't mean to do it... you just got it wrong."

With those words, my heart plummeted and I felt like the last and most important person in my life was giving up on me. He was preparing himself to lose me. An eerily similar idea to my long-held belief that I would eventually "get it wrong" and become a casualty of the disease of addiction. I had been thoroughly defeated and had no vigor left. My first thought was one of relief: "Good. I wouldn't want anyone to think I was suicidal." Then, the gravity of that thought sank in and I became acutely aware that my primary concern was not that I *would* die, but what other people would think about *how* I died. Then, the kairos moment happened, or what some might refer to as a spiritual awakening.

Abruptly, all of the hairs stood up on my head and I sat bolt upright, a well of intense energy rumbled deep inside of me. For a brief moment, all of the withdrawal symptoms vanished, and my parade of muddled thoughts became crystal clear. I screamed vehemently inside my head, "WHAT THE FUCK AM I DOING?!" All of my dreams, goals, ambitions, passions, unrealized potential, and future memories rose like angry skeletons who weren't yet ready to be buried. This was it – my ultimate breaking point. I finally found my place of true surrender and I laid down my shovel and stopped digging.

FREE AT LAST

"When I let go of what I am, I become what I might be."
— **Lao Tzu**

I never looked back after that day. I sought the medical assistance I needed and created a fantastic team of support around me. Initially, my friends and family were cautiously optimistic. They'd ridden the roller coaster with me attempting sobriety before and knew that the early days are especially turbulent and the risk of relapse is high. But it didn't take long for them to distinguish that this time was special. I had finally crossed the tightrope all the way to "acceptance" and, when I fully and honestly stopped fighting the disease, the most sensational thing happened. The desire to drink or take any substances was almost completely removed. For years now, I have had few temptations and I can comfortably be in social situations with alcohol present and not feel any unease.

However, my self-awareness is always on alert and I stay mindful that all it takes is one match to spark an explosion. This is only my experience, though. Every person in recovery has a different way of managing their sobriety that works best for them. Some choose to remove themselves completely from alcohol or drugs where possible; some struggle immensely with certain locations, people, or other "triggers" and make adjustments accordingly. I don't allow alcohol in my home, but otherwise, I don't feel a need to create restrictions.

With unconditional acceptance came the willingness to approach recovery and life in a different way because, admittedly, not many of my previous resolutions had worked. I had to throw out all of my stubborn ideas about what I thought I knew and become humble and teachable. Over time, I have extended the wisdom that I have acquired in sobriety to all other areas of my life and I practice the same guiding principles universally.

Every lesson I have learned, no matter how painful or unfair it may have felt at the time, I now view as a privilege. It's not our job to immerse ourselves in self-pity and plead, "Why me?" That's a waste of time. It is our duty to accept the circumstances placed before us and understand the message.

I feel exceptionally grateful now to have been blessed with the disease of addiction. Sometimes I wish it hadn't taken me 30 years of turmoil to get to that point, but that was the amount of time I needed. We have to live the content first before we can tell the story and we don't get to choose what our adversities in life will be or how long they will last for. Our power is in our perspective.

I have a disease where the treatment is continuous self-improvement. That's pretty cool. Most people spend their entire lives never truly leading themselves into the deep waters of their own potential. I've been graced with the motivation to make that a top priority every day – in fact, my life depends on it. And due to my dedication to constant growth and improvement, I have become a better wife, mother, friend, sister, mentor, student, teacher, leader, and influencer at the same time. Sheryl Sandberg says, *"When Option A is not available, go kick the shit out of Option B."* So, I do.

Every single day, I make a conscious choice to concentrate on what I can influence in my life and the world instead of what I can't, and I kick the shit out of it. I authentically and completely own who I am, accept my limitations, and pour my energy into enhancing my strengths. And that, *that*, is absolute freedom.

"Whatever your fate is, whatever the hell happens, you say, 'This is what I need.' It may look like a wreck, but go at it as though it were an opportunity, a challenge. If you bring love to that moment – not discouragement – you will find the strength there. Any disaster you can survive is an improvement in your character, your stature, and your life. What a privilege! This is when the spontaneity of your own nature will have a chance to flow. Then, when looking back at your life, you will see that the moments which seemed to be great failures, followed by wreckage, were the incidents that shaped the life you have now. You'll see this is really true. Nothing can happen to you that is not positive. Even though it looks and feels at the moment like a negative crisis, it is not. The crisis throws you back, and when you are required to exhibit strength, it comes."

—**Joseph Campbell**

CHAPTER THREE

CRUISING ALTITUDE

*"One can have no smaller or greater mastery
than mastery of oneself."*

— **Leonardo da Vinci**

MASTER OF YOUR HOUSE

As I built up weeks, months, and years of time sober, I launched myself on my journey toward self-mastery. One of my defining characteristics, being an alumna of the school of addiction, is that I do not do anything moderately. I am a person of extremes, period. If I'm in, I'm all in. So, when I undertook a commitment to improving every fiber of my being, it was serious business.

Roger Gabriel's "4 Steps to Self-Mastery" was one inspiration. To be the master of yourself is to fully appreciate your uniqueness. It entails taking complete responsibility for your own life – and that means all of it – the good, the bad, and the downright putrid. The first step is to become cognizant of who you are. Only with complete awareness and understanding can you begin to master the strengths and talents that you inherently possess. Needless to say, this is a lifelong and self-directed journey that unfolds in real time and whose progress can only be determined by you.

You can't speed up self-mastery, but you can maximize the journey with practice. The more you practice anything, the more proficient you become. The term practice doesn't only mean the action that you take, it also requires regularity. Without consistency and dedication, there can be no mastery. This is true for mastery of anything – a skill, a subject, an attitude, a sport, an instrument, or a language. What is unparalleled about mastery of the self is that you are zoning in on the central control center, which influences everything you touch. Capture the castle and the province will be yours. This is the great victory of self-mastery.

Self-mastery also requires patience, sincerity, purity, integrity, and self-belief. Patience is for acceptance of things as they are and to know when to step back and allow things to unfold in their own way and time. Sincerity is not only your words and actions with others, but honesty with yourself. Purity is the way you care for your body through your lifestyle: a healthy diet, regular exercise, and adequate sleep. Integrity is striving to be your best self, with honesty and honor. Self-belief is trusting yourself that you will handle whatever you uncover as you trudge the path of self-discovery and loving yourself through the process.

So, where's a good place to begin navigating the road to self-mastery? Start with awareness. Awareness is the foundation for everything. When I talk later in this book about being BADASS every day, it's exactly that – all six parts of the framework (the acronym) should be practiced every day to get the most value out of it, and all of the parts hinge on awareness.

Your thoughts are continuously swinging you into the past or the future, therefore, this is likely where you spend most of your life – reflecting about yesterday or predicting tomorrow – and unintentionally disconnected from today. To be aware is to be present, in this moment, right now. To practice awareness is to consciously drag yourself back from your past or future wanderings to what is happening now. To be aware is to witness your thoughts, emotions, actions, and what is occurring around you with detachment.

Visualize yourself blowing a wand of bubbles. You become quickly attuned to how hard you need to blow to release the perfect chain of bubbles. Now that they are all up in the air, just observe them. Resist the urge to be a two-year-old and catch them. Notice the perfection of the spherical shape, the fragility, and the iridescence. Then, pay attention to each one as they pop and disappear. Maybe one lands intact and lingers for a few seconds before popping, but they all pop. Now, imagine that those bubbles are your thoughts and emotions. This is awareness. The ability to simply observe from an external perspective, from your higher self, without pouncing on the urge to control or dominate the situation. You can't prevail over bubbles or you'll kill them – just let them be. The same holds true for thoughts and emotions. They don't stick around long, but we can learn an awful lot by paying attention to them and what they tell us. When we jump in and try to rule over them, we deprive ourselves of the message.

Awareness is one of the core skills of emotional intelligence and I was in love with that concept long before I set sail on my quest toward self-mastery. Or, as I say, from my "BS days" (before sobriety). Pun absolutely intended.

EMOTIONAL INTELLIGENCE

I first became familiar with emotional intelligence (EI or EQ) while I was at university in 1998, when EI was in its early days of research. I loved all kinds of self-improvement and psychology tools that helped me understand myself and how to change or improve certain aspects of my life. I was also interested in understanding other people and what their motivators and drivers were. Nestled underneath our personalities and surface behaviors lie a host of challenges that are common to most people: coping with stress, making good choices in life and career, dealing with conflict, creating sustainable and meaningful relationships, finding direction and purpose, creating a positive identity, etc. I wanted to learn how to do those things better. I found I really loved studying people and behaviors as a general subject and directed a lot of my university elective classes toward psychology and sociology.

Emotional intelligence was the new kid on the block in the world of behavioral science and had me particularly intrigued. It wasn't your typical fluffy rah-rah pop psychology stuff. It challenged the traditional notion that a person's IQ was the standard of excellence in life and gave scientific evidence about emotional regulation in our brains as a new way of thinking about the ingredients of life success. As someone who had been positively categorized by my determined IQ since I was a small child, I certainly didn't feel like I had excelled in life up to that point because of it. EI suggested there was more to our ability to be successful than just how capable we were of scoring highly on a test. I also could privately admit to myself that I did not have a good grip on my emotions most of the time. I was a loose cannon, a slave to my impulses, made poor decisions based on emotion, and had low confidence and self-respect. But the research on EI was still quite lean in the late 1990s, so my intrigue stayed on the back burner until 2014 when I became reacquainted with EI through my professional coaching work. I made a decision soon after EI came back into my world to increase my competency and become a specialist in emotional intelligence.

I obtained my certification as an Emotional Intelligence Practitioner through Genos International and immediately got involved with their global practitioner network. As I dove into guiding businesses on how to build emotionally intelligent cultures through coaching and facilitation, I simultaneously became aware of the positive influence that emotional intelligence was having on my personal life.

One of the many outstanding things about emotional intelligence is that, when we actively develop it, we can see huge impacts on our capacity for empathy, how we make decisions, how we communicate and collaborate with people, and how we inspire performance – not only in teams or businesses – but in ourselves. In a nutshell, I was literally taking my work home with me and it was boosting my life in so many ways: my relationships, the way I parented, and the way I understood and managed myself.

My personal journey of active recovery and self-mastery and my professional journey of enhancing emotional intelligence in businesses were parallel and complementary roads. Both roads focus heavily on self-awareness as the primary core skill. I was doing great with self-awareness at this point. I loved the process of self-discovery and being rigorously honest with myself wasn't something I shied away from anymore. I hungered for it. However, I wasn't thrilled about my self-assessment in another area. I struggled with the control and management of my emotions, specifically anger.

THE ONE YOU FEED

A grandfather is talking with his grandson.
The grandfather says, "In life, there are two wolves inside of us
which are always at battle.
One is a good wolf which represents things like kindness,
bravery, and love.
The other is a bad wolf which represents things like greed,
anger, and fear."
The grandson stops and thinks about it for a second then he looks
up at his grandfather and says, "Grandfather, which one wins?"
The grandfather replies, "The one you feed."

Nothing is a limitation unless you choose for it to limit you. If you do not confront the personal issues that keep you from being your best self, then you are making a decision to block your own way. I chose to not look too deeply at my own emotional triggers that sparked anger in me and the impact they had on my actions. I was so passionate about teaching others about the skills of emotional self-control and self-management, yet I privately struggled with it myself. I felt like a fraud. I lived with a constant undercurrent of anxiety and unproductive emotions every day. It had always been there, but drugs or alcohol had been the faithful crutch that I had leaned on to temper my temper. Now, the crutch was gone and I had not put any healthy or productive behaviors in its place, nor explored the underlying root issues. I was left with an emotional gaping hole. Irritation and agitation seemed to flavor everything I did and, on more occasions than I would like to admit, anger got the better of me and I would act out by slamming doors, hitting steering wheels, screaming at people, and cursing. I didn't feel good about myself when I was in this mode, but I couldn't seem to control it.

The way I explain it is that when you stop engaging in any destructive pattern or behavior (e.g. excessive work, television, food, alcohol, drugs, the internet, shopping, or something else), you take away the coping mechanism, but you're not actually addressing the problem by doing that. You're just taking off the bandage. The wound still needs care. Until you address the core issue, you're going to live with the disease. If you think of disease as *dis*-ease, I was in that state for quite some time. I was sober, but I was still feeling *dis*-ease.

I might have been able to conceal this in professional settings, but my ability to cope with strong emotions when I was alone or at home was impaired. When pressure, such as stress, builds and there is no release for it, we can experience an "amygdala hijack" where we become extremely and unnecessarily reactive and sensitive to events and situations. That heightened sensitivity caused my reactions to overheat the anger gauge. I had to look deep inside and ask myself a crucial question, *"How long do I want to continue feeling like this?"*

The other thing that I had to take into consideration was the chemical rush that I was getting from outbursts of anger. While the emotion of anger triggers intense physiological stress, accompanied by things like muscle tension, headaches or an increased heart rate, it reduces your psychological *distress*. When you get mad you secrete adrenaline, which biochemically makes you feel stronger. Additionally, and paradoxically, when you react to any felt provocation with anger, neurochemically you're also priming yourself for self-soothing. Therefore, when you get angry, you produce not only adrenaline but also *nor*-adrenaline, which has sedating properties.[9] I knew I had to find something to take anger's place that would mimic some of the perceived benefits I felt.

I have naturally high energy levels. I dislike sitting still for any prolonged period of time. I get fidgety when going to the movies or during long drives. When I fly, I try to always reserve an aisle seat so I can get up and move at will. I am also drawn to high-risk and high-adrenaline activities.

Several years ago, I was at an amusement park with my husband, son, and sister. I was in a rotten mood that day and no matter how hard I tried to adjust how I felt, I couldn't get rid of my clenched jaw and snappy sarcasm. Everything was irritating me – the crowds, the heat, my child's messiness and the lack of available napkins – everything. Most of our energy was spent on the kiddie rides and making sure my son was enjoying his experience. There was one hair-raising ride that appealed to me and the line was quite short, probably because there weren't too many brave souls willing to put themselves in the required peril. I challenged the others to join me. My sister looked at me like I was insane and agreed to hang out with my son while I dragged my reluctant husband into the ride's line. The ride looked like a giant tarantula and each arm rose up in the air one by one, with two seats tightly strapped to each arm. The arm would rotate high in the air, turn the seats upside down, and shake the passengers around like a snow globe. It was a recipe for screams of terror and flying vomit. I loved it. For the rest of the day, I bounced around the amusement park like a jubilant child with an enormous smile glued to my face. It became a bit of a running joke after that. If Nikki was in a bad mood, just turn her upside down and rattle her for a bit. Unfortunately, daily access to extreme thrill rides wasn't going to be the most practical mood stabilizer.

I was eager to try anything that was sensible to help calm my mind and reduce the tension that I was living with each day. Many people had suggested meditation, journaling, or yoga to me and I wasn't interested in those options. Remember, that "day spa-esque" calming, gentle vibe doesn't resonate with me – it heightens my agitation and impatience. Exercise was also a recommended option. I was a casual gym-goer at that point (meaning, I paid for the membership and attended once every few months out of guilt that I was paying for something that I was not using), but I was not really committed to, or interested in, exercise in any way. However, I did find that on the rare and mostly accidental occasions when I engaged in bursts of high-intensity exercise, I felt a substantial difference in my emotional stability. I wasn't thrilled about the idea, but logically it made a lot of sense to me to explore exercise further.

Starting to exercise when you have limited fitness ability is an extremely difficult process. No matter what your motivation is – mental health, weight loss, whatever – it's a hard slog that should not be underestimated, but always applauded. I imagine that many people have a great understanding of how challenging the initial stages of a fitness regime are and the incredible temptation to give up at every possible opportunity. The thing is, behavior change of any kind will only happen when the consequences of keeping the old behavior outweigh the uncertainty of adopting the new behavior. I adamantly did not want to be Little Miss Fiery anymore; I wanted to authentically practice what I preached about emotional self-management, so I embarked on the arduous journey toward channeling my peppery spirit in a healthy, sweaty way.

I started exploring with various kinds of exercises, apps, going to the gym regularly, taking classes, trying all sorts to burn off the anxiety and unproductive emotions and achieve a sense of calm. For a while, I was content with my efforts. I was trending in the right direction – my baseline irritation dropped a few degrees and I started sleeping better (insomnia is a common consequence of anxiety and trapped emotional energy). I made friends with the elliptical trainer and stationary bike, experimented with basic strength training, and put some focus on increasing my flexibility. Running was never on the cards. In fact, I detested the thought of running. I could be convinced to try a lot of activities, but I drew the line at running. In elementary school, I faked having exercise-induced asthma so I could get a doctor's exemption from P.E. class. So, while my classmates ran endless laps around the track, I hung out alone in the library and studied Beethoven's life or memorized passages by Plato.

LOVE POTION NO. 9

It began with a lie. As I got physically fitter and felt increasingly harmonious, I became curious to see what else I was capable of. It's in my nature to always up the ante. I do this in all sorts of constructive and destructive ways. Sometimes that tendency can pay off wonderfully, like in professional and educational achievements, and other times I push too far and learn lessons via consequences. Whatever the situation, I don't stay content for long. The temptation to explore the next level is irresistible. It was time to get some better guidance from a trainer, rather than relying on my DIY efforts. I made an appointment for an initial assessment with a personal trainer to outline a balanced plan of strength training and cardio. She suggested that on the cardio days I run. She asked me, "How far can you run?" I mumbled, "10km" (6.2mi) but even as the words came out of my mouth, I knew that was a dumb thing to say. I had never run 10km in my life!

At that point, I was a smoker, I was just about to turn 40, and I could probably run 1km (0.62mi) if I was lucky. But based on what I told her, she suggested that I run 10km three times a week. I thought that suggestion was completely nuts like, "People actually do that?" I ultimately decided to be honest with myself and a tad more realistic about my current fitness abilities. I liked the idea of running 10km, or maybe I just got stuck on the fact that I *claimed* I could so I inadvertently created a challenge with myself, but I didn't want to actually put in the effort to be able to do it. It was just a nice idea. My cousin suggested that I try a Couch to 5K (3.1mi) app because, never being a runner in my entire life, it was not going to be sensible to just go out and attempt to run 10km. I also wanted to quit smoking at that time. I'd given up everything else (including meat, dairy, and sugar) but that was the last vice I was still clinging to. I thought, "All right. I'll do this Couch to 5K app," and I figured that might also give me the incentive to stay off the cigarettes as well. However, my mindset stayed completely fixed that I was going to hate every minute of it. For the next few weeks, I built up my ability to run and I was eventually able to run the 5km without stopping. I was pleased with that, but I still detested running. I simply could not understand why some people were so passionate about it.

Once I could run 5km, I kept thinking about that conversation I had with the trainer about 10km. I never did engage with her further after that initial assessment. My dishonesty prevented me from wanting to commit to a relationship with her, so I continued on my DIY fitness plan. One ambitious day I thought, "Well, why not? Let's see if I can do it." I didn't think that being able to run 10km was going to be any more enjoyable than 5km, maybe just twice the pain. But my itch to increase the stakes wasn't going away. What have I got to lose? I figured it might take roughly the same amount of time to go from 5km to 10km as it had zero to 5km, so I focused on pushing the distance out bit by bit. Then, one day I was almost back home, just shy of 8km (5mi), when the magic happened.

I use the visual of cassette tapes playing in my head. Whenever I decide to go for a run, my brain inserts a Greatest Hits compilation in my mental cassette player. The tape is called "The Anthology of Excuses and Reasons to Stop." When I get dressed and lace up for my run, I press play, and it sounds like this: "It's cold outside. It's raining. I'm tired. I didn't sleep well. I have work to do. My toe hurts." Right? I'm certain you have your own version of that anthology. I actually visualize that tape in motion. I see the hubs slowly turning and the tape moving from the supply reel to the take-up reel through the window. The good thing about cassette tapes is that they have a start and an end; eventually they will run out. They don't have a shuffle or repeat. They just go from start to finish. Looking back now, I fully understand why I never had an interest in running. It was because I always stopped running before the tape ran out, so all I heard was the negativity and the excuses, thus reinforcing how much I disliked the process.

On this day when the magic happened, it was February 2018, only a couple of months after I started running for the first time ever. I was nearly home when I suddenly became aware that I felt light and energetic. It was a completely different feeling. The fatigue was gone and I felt fresh, like I had just started my run. I looked at my tracker and I was at about the 8km mark, which was the farthest distance I had ever run in my life. I was steps away from my apartment building and routine was pulling me to stop, but that day, I thought, "No. I don't want to stop right now. I don't know what this feeling is, but I like it." So, I kept going. I went for about another 6km (3.72mi) beyond that. I could not believe how easy those last 6kms were. They felt completely different to the first 8km, and different from any run I'd ever done before. I transformed from a clunky elephant to a *Chariots of Fire* poster girl.

Looking back on it, what stands out to me was the mental freedom. I can't remember what my knees felt like, or my ankles or my hips, but I remember that the excuses stopped. The tape stopped playing.

All of the negative messages and self-defeating talk, plus the constant drone of anxiety that occupied the driver's seat in my mind, went silent. All I could feel was the wind on my face, the steady rhythm of my breath, and the blood coursing through my veins.

What was this? I was stricken by a love potion on that run. It shook me to my core. Running. Me? Seriously. I felt superhuman, stronger, and more graceful than I could ever remember feeling before. If a cheetah had strode up alongside of me at that moment, I would have glanced at her with a hint of a smile and a knowing nod that assured, "We got this."

CHAPTER FOUR

OH, THE PLACES YOU'LL GO!

"You have brains in your head. You have feet in your shoes. You can steer yourself in any direction you choose. You're on your own. And you know what you know. You are the guy who'll decide where to go."

— **Dr. Seuss,** *Oh, the Places You'll Go!*

RUNNER'S HIGH

After that unplanned 14km (8.7mi) run, I spent the next day mentally unglued. I wanted to analyze the heck out of that run and try to understand what had changed on a biological and chemical level. I listed all of the variables that might have played a role in the performance shift; what, when, and how much I had eaten, hydration, sleep pattern, stress level, shoes, and any other contributing factor. I also wanted to dismiss it as a fluke. I hated running and all my evidence to date supported that conclusion. *Don't you dare bring me new information that might suggest otherwise and force me to reconsider my position!* More than anything, I felt perplexed, like a superhero who had just woken up after their life-changing event and realized that they suddenly had powers that weren't there before. I wanted to explore that feeling again – that light, confident, fit, and free feeling.

Indeed, I'd call it a high, but it wasn't the kind of high that I was familiar with. There was no massive and sudden rush with an equally dramatic plummet that concluded with a lower finishing point than when you started. This feeling, this "runner's high," was a slow and steady onset with a gradual drop that concluded a long time later with a much higher finishing point than the starting point. Personally, I think the term "runner's high" is grossly overrated and misunderstood. There is a lot of science comparing the changes that occur in the body and brain during exercise to the processes that occur with drug use. This book is not about that science. Suffice it to say that an apple is not at all like a banana. If you enjoy fruit, you may appreciate both, but it's unlikely that you will get the two confused.

Like any good academic who appreciates theory but requires data to be convinced, I had one objective: test every hypothesis. For weeks I ran by feel, not following any specific program or guidelines, and tracked every run to collect the data. I rapidly figured out that I was attracted to the longer distances and that was primarily due to those negative tapes that I played. I wanted to outrun the tapes and observe if there were consistent patterns in what tape played (i.e. what negative thoughts came up and how frequently), how many kilometers did the tape play for, and if there were any noteworthy variables. Because my motivation with running at this point was about managing unproductive emotions, I focused on how to run to achieve that optimum state of mental calmness. I tried to not view running as a sprint or a hard workout. I was more curious about what was going to feel the best, so I was happy to go slower and longer so I could really explore all the physical and mental awareness that happened during the run. Physically, I responded to running efficiently. My body type is short and light and I had no previous injuries or medical hurdles to cross, so once I started to acclimate my mindset, my physical condition adapted quickly.

I also found that running was proving to be a remarkably effective way of controlling the anger and anxiety tendencies that I had felt so trapped by. I felt a steady calm on the days that I ran and my emotional swings were much less severe overall.

THE FIRST HALF

Less than a month after my magical 14km run, I ran my first half marathon distance (21.1km/13.1mi). It was slow and awkward, but I did it. That was three months after my 40th birthday. Going from someone who was an unfit middle-aged smoker to running a half marathon in three months made me incredibly proud and further, made me wonder, *"What else can I do?"* Plus, I was completely hooked on the sport now. I soaked up as much information as I could about training techniques, gear, injury-prevention, and optimal nutrition. It was ironic to think that something I was absolutely convinced that I hated could turn into something that I loved so quickly. It was like I always had a hidden runner inside of me, but I just had to be patient and open-minded long enough to discover that she was there.

> *"You've always had the power my dear, you just had to learn it for yourself."*
> — **Glinda,** *The Wizard of Oz*

It was in these early days of running that I really started to dig deep and go further with self-mastery and potential. I already had the perfect trifecta of personal development happening with active sobriety, emotional intelligence in my work life, and my pursuit of self-mastery. Running added another dimension to my thought patterns about potential and gave me a practical way to explore myself on new levels. Over the last few years, I have spent countless hours pounding the pavement pondering big topics, igniting my own curiosity, and absorbing information to answer one question: *"What does it take to become our most powerful self?"*

After breaking through the half marathon distance barrier on my own, the urge to enter a race crept up. Competition is one of my most dominant strengths and something that has always been a defining characteristic of mine. My competitive streak has come out to play in many healthy ways over the years, especially with academic competition. My best friend in university was equally as academically competitive and we sniffed each other out early in our first term together. Our strong desire to outscore each other pushed us both to study harder and certainly had a positive impact on our grades, but it also strengthened our friendship.

That competitive inclination has also not served me well, say with drinking games, where my mind might have been fiercely determined to outdrink a man twice my size but my body refused to cooperate. It can also be disheartening for someone with a strong competitive spirit to admit that many people are not competitive at all and don't appreciate efforts to engage with them in that way. I find this especially true in workplaces. It might pay off in some instances, but you are likely to make more enemies than friends if you give off a bloodhound vibe – particularly with a superior.

I equally love being competitive with myself and I have found many creative ways to do that over the years, but once I started running, a magical measuring tool was handed to me. I hadn't run my first race yet, but I could have told you with absolute certainty that I was going to take to that environment like a fish to water.

RUN MELBOURNE 2018

My first race. There was nothing strategic or sentimental about why I selected this race as my first. It just happened to be the next upcoming half marathon on the local race calendar. I followed a training plan, took on board all the advice I read about how to prepare for a race, and my excitement was like a kid at Christmas. On race day, I woke up in the middle of the night to get my breakfast in a few hours earlier and got dressed in the living room so I wouldn't wake my husband or son. Guided by the glow of streetlights, I walked to the start line (I was fortunate to live close enough to walk) before dawn with butterflies in my stomach and chattering teeth. The temperature was near freezing.

I found my corral and copied what I saw some others doing – light stretches, lunges, jogging in place – as we waited to move toward the start line. Having no racing experience, I didn't have an expectation of time, but I made a flexible goal to finish in under two hours. I didn't know what variables I would meet on the course, but 2:00hrs would be about a 5:40min/km pace and I knew I could do that. One thing I have not done in any race so far is start too fast and blow out early. I try to train to negative splits on most of my longer runs (where the second half of your run is faster than the first half) so I'm most comfortable settling into my groove, letting other racers make the overeager mistake of launching off the line, overtaking them later, and finishing strong. That's a pattern that has worked for me so far.

Right from the start line, I loved every minute of this race. I soaked in the atmosphere. I was completely in my element. I felt energized by the 5,000 other runners on the course with me. I marveled at the massive crowds lining the streets, cheering, holding signs, and handing out sugary snacks to the runners. There were bands playing, spectators dressed in outrageous costumes, cheerleaders performing, and even some of the police officers patrolling the course were shouting words of encouragement. It was one of the greatest displays of community support I had ever witnessed. The words of Kathrine Switzer (the first woman to run the Boston Marathon in 1967) echoed in my head, *"If you are losing faith in human nature, go out and watch a marathon."*

I held a steady pace until about the 18km (11.2mi) mark and then it was time to step it up for a strong finish. Except, I realized I had a slight dilemma. I had to pee. I had probably drunk too much water before the race and it was catching up with me now. I checked my watch and I was on track to sub-two (hours), but I didn't have much room to spare. Every porta potty that I had passed had a line, too. As much as I disliked the idea, my competitive instincts took charge and I concluded that my finishing time was more important to me than wetting myself.

With that decision firmly made, I kicked my effort into high gear to close out my last 3km and crossed the finish line at 1:58:13. I was ecstatic. I was uncomfortable and slightly insecure about the large wet patch hugging the inside of my tights, but hey, this was a race and I assured myself that I was not the first person to cross a finish line somewhat self-conscious. Any sheepishness that I felt was overpowered by the weight of the medal around my neck. A symbol of bravery, grit, perseverance, and patience; my heart soared with pride in all that medal represented. I looked around me with equal glory at the community of people gathered together at the finish line in celebration of their own relentless pursuit of excellence. I knew without any doubt that this half marathon was going to be my first of many races to come. I had found more than just a sport that I could compete in – I awoke a passion. When you discover something that you are truly passionate about, protect it, respect it, and own it. You owe it to yourself to never let your passion take a backseat. It is through your passions that your soul speaks.

I sometimes catch myself wondering what my life would have been like if I had engaged in sports at an earlier age. I have all the markings of a competitive athlete and might have been phenomenal in my prime years. Then I remind myself that that is not the story I was destined to tell. This is. People can spend entirely too much time lost in a storyline that is not theirs. When we immerse ourselves in the "woulda, shoulda, couldas" we deny our authentic purpose. Sure, things could have gone much differently *"if only..."* Everyone can play that narrative in their heads, but that is fantasy and it doesn't change reality. Look at your feet. That is where you are. That is the only script you can affect right now. The only question should be: *What are you going to do with it?*

BIBS, BELTS, AND MEDALS

The next two years were dominated by training and racing. I wanted to experience as much as I could, learn as fast as possible, and keep improving. I was fitter than I had ever been in my life and I felt amazing and fully in control. True to my nature, I was all in and my growth as an athlete accelerated quickly. Between 2018 and 2020, I ran 21 races of varying lengths: one ultramarathon, three marathons, six half marathons, and eleven miscellaneous shorter distances, stair climbs, and obstacle courses. Twice, I finished in the top ten for my category (gender + age group).

Once I had a few official times under my soles, I started to put more emphasis on speed and doing better than my previous best. As much as I enjoy competing against others, I am even more motivated by pushing myself and seeing continuous improvement. I love the granular nature of running as well. There are so many intricate levels of fine-tuning that can be applied to maximize performance and objective data that can be collected and analyzed. That kind of scrutiny is alluring to my inner-nerd.

In addition to running, in 2018, I started training in Kyokushin karate as well and I continue to train in both sports. Karate came into the picture through my son. Then nine years old, I wanted to get my son involved with karate classes on the weekends to assist him with improving his fitness, focus, and discipline. I was thrilled to find a fabulous dojo near where we lived with an excellent culture, headed by one of the world's most respected shihan (master instructor or head of the organization) of the style. My son was cautious and needed a lot of coaxing to try the karate classes. At this dojo, the classes on the weekends are mixed adults and children, so there are a number of families who train together. I told my son that I would never ask him to do anything that I wasn't willing to do myself, a core value that had been instilled in me by my father, so I enrolled myself in classes with him. Training with my son on weekends is one of my most treasured activities with him.

Similar to running, if I hadn't been open-minded and willing to try karate, I never would have realized how much I liked it. During the week, the adult students train more seriously so I've moved up in the ranks, compete in interclub tournaments, and dedicate a percentage of my overall weekly training to karate. Personally, I find karate a lot more challenging than running because of its complexity and requirement of coordination. Coordination is not a strength of mine, but perseverance is, so I keep showing up and improving – one block, one kick, one strike at a time. Karate and running also complement each other wonderfully for cross-training. Running makes me a better fighter because of my endurance and general fitness ability. Karate makes me a better runner because the range and speed of motion required strengthens my body in ways that running alone cannot achieve.

As far as emotional self-management is concerned, both running and karate have proven to be extremely effective for me. Both provide catharsis in their own way. Running allows me deep introspection and thought because I run alone, often for hours at a time, so I have the ability to view situations from multiple perspectives and fully consider options before choosing how to respond – the most powerful pause. Karate requires complete focus on the task at hand and a clearing of the mind. If I am ruminating about something and not mentally present, I am likely to get injured, injure someone else, or at best, mess up the rhythm of my training partners.

Now, when I facilitate workshops on emotional self-management and resilience, instead of feeling like a walking paradox, I tell stories about my own previous struggles with anger and anxiety and how I conquered them as an example of how that competency can be developed – and as a lesson about authenticity.

ADMIRATION VS. INSPIRATION

"Ninety-nine percent of failures come from people who have a habit of making excuses."
— **George Washington Carver**

One of the greatest privileges of being a mature-age novice athlete is that I have the opportunity to demonstrate to men and women that age is a fact, not an excuse. You don't have to *be* an athlete to *become* an athlete. In fact, that statement could represent anything if you replace the word athlete with a noun of your choice: expert, musician, leader, writer, etc. One of the most common excuses I hear from mature adults about starting anything new is, "I'm too old for that!" or some variation of this, but usually citing age as a rationalization. The trouble with this is that if you become good at making excuses you won't be good at anything else. Excuses are the tools that people use to build unhappiness.

When I began running at 40, in no way did I imagine that I would go from zero to ultramarathon in two and a half years. I've suffered plenty with imposter syndrome during that process and still feel a little bit uneasy being called, or referring to myself as, an athlete. However, I am aware that this is based on a limiting belief that "athletes" are younger or have had a sporting history in their younger years. Aside from feeling like I don't meet the prerequisites for the label, I have not felt the urge to use my later start as an excuse for inaction or surrender. As Harry S. Truman expressed, *"Imperfect action is better than perfect inaction."*

It is possible that I have had to manage a few injuries that my 20-year-old self wouldn't have been confronted with and, as athletes increase in maturity, they are wise to make adjustments in their training for natural evolutions, such as decreased flexibility and longer recovery time. But a large number of people will use excuses and comparisons to stop themselves before they ever begin. One of the ways that I prevent my age from ending up on a menu of justifications is to understand the difference between admiration and inspiration.

Admiration is who you look at with appreciation and maybe awe, but don't necessarily want to model yourself after. For example, I have deep respect and admiration for Eliud Kipchoge who, in 2019, became the first human to run a marathon in under two hours. But running a sub two-hour marathon will never be a goal of mine. So, I admire him for his achievements and the positive attention he has brought to the sport of marathon running, but I don't internalize that.

Someone else who I admire and who is a bit closer to me, is my friend Sean Bell. Sean is a superb ultra-endurance runner who is currently making huge waves as an athlete and motivational speaker. He has completed several 24-hour runs, 50 marathons in 50 days, and many other sporting achievements that blow my mind – with even bigger plans for the future. He is also in his 20s and has been an athlete of several sports for many years. I am in frequent contact with him so I know how Sean trains, how long it takes him to recover, and so on. I admire him, but have to be careful to not mentally compare my training with his or I might get some distorted perceptions of what capacity and recovery look like which could lead me to feel discouraged, or perhaps overtrain.

Inspiration, on the other hand, is where there's a change *in* you. It *in*spires you to do something within yourself, such as getting energized by someone's journey or accomplishments that causes you to make positive choices and take action in your own life. As a mature runner, I am selective in who I choose for inspiration. I look for athletes who have travelled a similar path to me, and are a little bit farther down that road.

Rich Roll is an example of an athlete who inspires me. Rich and I have a lot of similarities in our stories. We have complementary nutrition philosophies and he's a recovering alcoholic who also started running at 40. Now, he's an ultra-endurance athlete in his 50s. I look at him with inspiration because I see how so many of his experiences reflect what I have been through, where I'm at now, and what is possible in front of me.

Sinead Diver is another runner who inspires me. At 41, she won the 2018 Melbourne Marathon with a time that set a new course record and earned her the fastest Australian female marathon runner aged 40+. She had only been running for eight years at that point, having commenced the sport in 2010 after having her first child. That inspires me because, again, it helps me to see what is conceivable for me now, not a past version of me.

Another example is Jeannie Rice. In her 70s, she's a world record holder in her age group for both the marathon and half marathon. So, I examine my journey and think, "Okay. I started at 40, but by the time I'm in my 70s, I'll be a 30+ year veteran of running," and I start to witness the potential unfold.

Where can you apply admiration vs. inspiration in your life? Maybe it's not with a sport, but with a professional goal. Who are the people in your industry that you feel are successful? What does their context look like? Do you admire them at arm's length, or do they cause a change *in* you, an *in*spiration.

In my work as a speaker, I look to the professionals who have gotten millions of views on their TED Talks with admiration. I can study their technique and delivery and soak up a lot of insights from their performance, but I must also remain mindful of what has gotten them to that point (and aware that I do not know what 99% of their quest has been like) and not allow my mind to wander into unhelpful comparisons.

For inspiration, I look at other speakers who have had similar training to me but have been speaking longer or with greater success and learn from their experience to make positive choices for my next career goals. Who you choose for inspiration should be people who have walked in your shoes and who understand where you are in your journey because they've been there.

I'm proud of my running achievements so far, and when I think of the big picture, I know I started at just the right time. I haven't come this far to only go this far. Perspective is either your gas pedal or your brake pedal – the choice is yours.

PEEKING DOWN THE ULTRA RABBIT HOLE

"Only those who will risk going too far can possibly find out how far one can go."
— T. S. Eliot

After completing my third marathon in 12 months, I wanted to stretch myself to the next level and see what else I was capable of. By that point, I was confident in my ability to run 42.2km (26.2mi). I had completed that distance three times in competition and had come close several times in training. I was intrigued by the world of ultramarathon racing and wanted to test my mettle and see what else I was made of beyond the marathon length. An ultramarathon can be any distance that is further than the traditional marathon. They can range from under 50km (31mi) to ridiculous lengths of hundreds or thousands of kilometers/miles. I love the marathon distance and plan to continue to compete in them and improve my times, but it didn't surprise me that I wouldn't stay content at that level for long.

In December 2019, I registered to race in my first 60km (37.28mi) ultramarathon at the Great Ocean Road Running Festival in May 2020. I had just set a new PR/PB (Personal Record or Personal Best) at the Melbourne Marathon a few weeks before and felt like I was in good physical condition to increase my training over the next five months.

A SENSIBLE TRADE?

Naturally, this ultramarathon announcement worried some people who feared that I was trading one addiction for another. I understood and didn't fault their concerns. Many endurance sports see an unusually high percentage of former addicts in their participants. There is a strong attraction there for people whose brains are hardwired for extremes.

When someone's behavior has been so extreme on the negative side, chances are high that they might seek out extremes on the positive side. That tendency to gravitate toward the edge has more to do with that individual's comfort with being an outlier than it does with "addiction." It can be difficult for someone who prefers more moderation in their life to comprehend that. The part of the brain that pushes us to the finish line of an endurance race is also the same part that can behave self-destructively. It's determination: the resolve to keep going long after everyone else has stopped. There is no difference in the competency, rather it's how you choose to use that strength that will determine whether it's constructive or destructive.

That doesn't mean that having an addictive mind will make you a more successful endurance runner. There are extraordinary athletes and tough-as-nails competitors from every walk of life dominating the sport. It's about acknowledging that there is a positive side to any seemingly negative variable. There is also a level of accountability and pride that athletes experience when they engage in healthy competition against themselves or others. It's easier to get into productive mindset patterns like, "Two months ago, I couldn't run five kilometers, and now I can run ten. What else can I do?" Exercise of any kind provides people with a sense of empowerment and mental fortitude. The measurable and tangible ways athletes can track their progress may be as important to addicts as anyone.

When I was actively feeding my addictions, I couldn't trust myself to uphold any commitments and I constantly let myself and others down. Now as an endurance runner, I purposely put myself in tough situations, I tell myself that I trust myself and that I won't quit, and that internal strength carries me through to completion of my goal, time and time again. For a once hopeless addict, that determination is the most powerful drug.

Am I mindful about my tendency to take things *too* far? Absolutely, I have to be. I know my warning signs and I'm always on alert for them. However, I look at recovery and running independently. Running is wonderful and it helps me stay sober, but it's not a substitute for active sobriety. Sobriety requires a lifetime of commitment and work; a race with no finish line.

SCREECHING HALT

"Everything can be taken from a man but one thing: the last of the human freedoms — to choose one's attitude in any given set of circumstances, to choose one's own way."
— Viktor Frankl

Eight weeks before race day, in March 2020, the world came to an abrupt standstill due to COVID-19. I was heavily engaged with my training plan and in the midst of all the initial uncertainty, I kept running. In fact, that training plan was a huge security blanket for me. The world was in shock with scatterbrained businesses and governments changing the rules daily because no one knew how to handle the crisis that had befallen us. My training plan became my only constant. No matter what the latest news headlines were, I knew that today I was running 32km and tomorrow 19km, and so forth. I relied on that one piece of sanity when nothing else made sense.

As anticipated, the Great Ocean Road race was cancelled, along with just about every sporting event in the foreseeable future, including the Tokyo Olympics. Shockwaves were felt in sporting communities across the world and I was faced with a choice: continue with my training plan or take my foot off the gas and relax a bit? Taking the local government advice at that time into consideration (no restrictions on running solo outdoors), I decided that I would proceed with my training and, on the day of the cancelled race, run 60km out my front door. I proclaimed, "They can cancel my race, but they cannot cancel my feet."

This was a surprisingly easy decision to make. Sure, I was disappointed. I love the whole race experience, the crowds, the fanfare, and the celebration. But I was still determined and willing to continue with my intention of running my first ultramarathon by myself, without all the public excitement. That resolve solidified that the hunger to achieve that goal came from my core, an authentic desire to test my own limits for my own fulfillment, as opposed to being dependent on external influences to stay motivated.

On the day that would have been race day, true to my promise, I headed out the front of my apartment building and started to run. My husband accompanied me on a bike with a backpack carrying all the hydration, energy, and medical supplies I might need. There would be no aid stations and due to COVID-19, I wanted to be fully self-contained. Before we left home, I asserted to my husband, "I am allowed to scream. I am allowed to cry. I am NOT allowed to quit." I pressed him to give me his word that he understood that. I ran 30km (18.6mi) in one direction, turned around and headed home. All was fine for that first half and at my turnaround point I was still vibrant and full of life. It just felt like a typical training long run.

Then, I started to feel a nagging pain in my ankle. I stopped a couple of times to adjust my shoe, thinking that it was the shoe that was the problem because I hadn't felt that particular pain before. At 42.2km (26.2mi) when I passed the marathon distance, I took a mental note and rejoiced, "Every step I take from this point forward is the farthest I've ever gone." I ran past the 53km (33mi) mark before I chose to walk for a bit. My ankle was really hurting and I was worried because I didn't know what the pain was telling me or how to manage it.

My husband got off his bike and walked alongside me in silence. After a few more kilometers of watching me wince and limp, he couldn't contain his pity and suggested, "Why don't you just ride the bike for the rest of the way? We're almost home. It's starting to get dark." I glared at him out of the corner of my eye. With the steadfast tenacity of a fighter who refuses to stay down, I hissed, "I will finish this on my own two feet."

As we approached our building and my 60km imaginary finish line, I felt numb. I wearily pulled my phone out of my pocket and tapped "End Workout." That was it. No cheering crowds, no overwhelming rush of adrenaline and elation bubbling to the surface, no squeals of joy, no medal triumphantly placed around my neck. The streets were quiet. All I wanted to do was quietly crawl into the bushes and throw up. I had nothing left to give.

The next day, with my legs perched up against the wall to relieve the fluid build-up, I cried for hours. All of the emotion of completing a huge goal that was completely self-driven came crashing down. I cried in anguish for the pain. I cried in sadness for the absence of the race. I cried in empathy for all of the other athletes who had been stripped of their events that they had trained so hard for. I cried in fear for the uncertainty of the world. I cried in satisfaction for my inner strength, my resilience, and my refusal to give up on myself when the universe would have let me off the hook. I cried in grief for my father, who had passed away only a few weeks before, and whose beams of pride I would no longer see. I cried in sorrow for the caterpillar that I once was. I cried in gratitude for the beauty of transformation. I cried because it was all worth it.

I couldn't wait to do it all over again.

I have a metal sign that hangs next to my bed with words I choose to be reminded of every day, especially when motivation plays the foe:

It will hurt.
It will take time.
It will require dedication.
It will require willpower.
You will need to make healthy decisions.
It requires sacrifice.
You will need to push yourself to the max.
There will be temptation.
But I promise you, when you reach your goal,
It's worth it.

TAPPING THE WELL

I have only begun to scratch the surface of all the possibilities that running offers and what potential I actually have as an athlete within the sport. I hope to be peeling back those layers of discovery for many years to come. But in the first few years of my running exploration, I tapped the well and, oh boy, did it flow.

You can learn an incredible amount and become truly inspired and fulfilled by what you observe externally from the other people around you. Some people can spend their whole lives engaging with life from a safe perch and be perfectly content with that. It takes real courage to open your own Pandora's box and take a peek inside. Most of the daunting stuff is inside of you.

Think of your soul as a vast well that contains every bit of data that has ever been collected about you.

At the surface of that well is your conscious life – your thoughts, opinions, experiences, memories, and accessible emotions. That's a nice place to explore – it's light, it's safe, and you can see everything clearly at the surface.

Down a bit deeper in the well is your unconscious life – your dreams, beliefs, intuitions, suppressed memories, values, and core identity. That's a bit more confronting because this is where you are faced with unfulfilled hopes and ambitions, plans that never happened, and past hurts. Many people choose not to visit there at all. Others will, but opt to not stay long or visit too often.

Go farther down the well and it gets medieval and dark. This is where the nasties hang out – your fears, repressed emotions, doubts, limiting beliefs, shame, and regrets. This is the stuff most people actively try to ignore.

Deeper still, so deep, is where your potential lives. Only people who are brave enough to travel through the other levels of the well will be capable of exploring the depths of their own potential.

My journey as a woman in recovery and as a runner have taught me an incredible amount about every level of my well, who I authentically am at my core, a tease of what I am capable of, and how to apply the lessons I have learned, either willingly or unwillingly, along the road to all other areas of my life. Every day, I am discovering more of what it takes to become my most powerful self.

My mission is to share with you the methods that I have used, to provide you with light as you travel down your own well to the depths of your unique potential, and to empower you to fully embrace and master the BADASS that you are – and become your most powerful self.

PART TWO

INTRODUCTION TO THE
BADASS FRAMEWORK

In Part One, I shared with you a peek into my personal journey and some of the events that have shaped me into the woman I am today. A lot of my story has been characterized by struggle, but from that struggle I have emerged stronger, wiser, and more powerful than I could have ever dreamed possible. I thank adversity and challenges for the lessons they have taught me. I thank grace and humility for allowing me to be teachable. I thank grit and resilience for the willingness to apply what I have learned and to never give up on myself.

At the root of most people's journey is struggle, as well. Our struggles come in many shapes, colors, and sizes, but it's the one common denominator we all share. Life is challenging and we struggle.

I developed my BADASS framework initially to help me navigate my own challenges. I desperately wanted to be the best version of myself, but quite often I didn't know what that looked like. We talk a lot about being our "best selves" – it's quite a popular catchphrase these days – but I haven't seen that idea come with an instruction manual on how to attain a "best version of self" status. So, I made my own blueprint for how to manage life's struggles, overcome my own setbacks and limiting beliefs, move forward with purpose and deliberate action, and elevate myself to unshakable, confident ground every single day.

Through the process of developing my framework I realized that being my "best self" wasn't a trophy I wanted to win anymore, because I had discovered the motherlode. By holding myself accountable to the BADASS model in everything I do, I have been able to access my most powerful self – and powerful is far superior to best. I hope you find as much value from the BADASS framework as I have.

It works. I would not recommend a program of action unless I had already seen ironclad results in my own life and truly inspiring outcomes from select coaching groups who have helped me refine the recommendations in each section based on their experiences.

The remainder of this book dives deep into each of the six letters of the BADASS acronym (B = Brave, A = Authentic, D = Direction, A = Action, S = Self-love, and S = Self-talk). They do not have to be applied in any specific order: each part stands alone and holds equal weight. However, you will see how all of the parts weave together and strengthen each other as well. My recommendation is to move through the model in whatever way feels right to you. There might be one specific area that you would like to focus on and enhance now. Then later on, something else might stand out for you. Or, you might choose to dive in and take several parts of the framework on board together. It all comes down to context and everybody's context is different.

Bravery demands action. It accepts risk and proceeds in spite of fear. Fear keeps us limited and stagnant; bravery moves us forward. You will miss every opportunity that you don't go after and this requires being courageous enough to make mistakes, look silly, fail, risk disapproval, or be rejected. It also takes great bravery to own and accept who you are – all of you, not just the parts you showcase for others.

Authenticity means that your thinking, your values, your words, and your actions are in alignment. It challenges us to explore what is important to us, how we want to show up, and how we want to influence those around us. Authenticity demands that you are consistent with your character and accept that others will do what they *see you do*, not what you *say to do*. Our level of authenticity is usually proportionate to the amount of trust others have in us.

Direction involves creating purpose and meaning in your life and leading from your heart. It's about pursuing your dreams with confidence and living a life that is driven forward by possibility, not fear. Having good direction also calls for agility because never does a path travel a straight line. We have seen in recent times that the ability to shift without losing direction is one of the most important skills we can cultivate.

Action is where everything begins and ends. Intentions do not lead to results, only actions do. Good action requires goals. Without having solid goals and a plan to get where you want to go, you will never arrive anywhere meaningful. It's about recognizing the power of choice and taking the steps to be a person of commitment, persistence, and endurance.

Self-love is the glue that holds it all together and the best investment you can ever make. How much we invest in caring for and respecting ourselves sets the tone for the amount of time and energy we can give to our business, family, and other relationships. You cannot fill from an empty cup, yet many of us strive valiantly to override science and end up suffering greatly.

And finally, **Self-talk** is where we find our greatest superpower. There is such potency in our self-talk that the way you think about yourself and the stories you tell yourself will influence your motivation, actions, and habits, and put you in complete control over your success. You will become what you tell yourself you are.

Are you ready?

CHAPTER FIVE

RISKY BUSINESS (BRAVE)

"He who is not every day conquering some fear has not learned the secret of life."

— **Ralph Waldo Emerson**

B ravery is risky business. It's a coincidence that the BADASS acronym starts with the letter "B," but it's appropriate since bravery is one of the primary characteristics of a badass. A person cannot engage their most powerful self or frolic on the playground of self-mastery without having bravery as part of their personal credo. Every great action, big or small, starts with a brave decision. Brave decisions carry some level of risk. Risk creates fear.

I asked my 11-year-old son, "What does it mean to be brave?" He pondered this question for a heartbeat and then replied, "Feeling scared but doing it anyway." I nodded, pleased with his succinct definition. Then I pensively journeyed down my own rabbit hole of wondering why adults have to overcomplicate everything. Bravery is simple: it's seeing the risk, feeling the fear, and doing it anyway.

Bravery requires us to act. So much of our fear is a result of our own blurred thinking and limiting beliefs. We replay negative tapes from our history that keep us in a risk-averse state. These old messages prevent us from making the big sale, applying for that new job, starting our own business, or simply standing up for ourselves. Most likely, the people who make the sale, get the job, start their own business, or stand up for themselves are, or were, just as scared as you. The difference is, they took action. They didn't let their fear stop them. They acted in spite of their fear. Fear is stagnant. Bravery is action.

Bravery requires us to rearrange our disorganized thinking and confront the limiting beliefs that have been holding us back. It insists that we examine our heart and not look for something from the outside to change us. Others can influence us but no one can help us move from fear to bravery. That is a heart decision. We must do that ourselves.

In this chapter we look at some of the ways bravery can be defined, with ideas on how you can apply more bravery to your life. What heart decisions are going to make a difference for you?

MISTAKING THE EXTRAORDINARY FOR THE ORDINARY

Bravery comes in many sizes, shapes, and forms. Many people do not feel that they demonstrate bravery because of how they internally define what qualifies as brave. When most people think of bravery their minds immediately envisage elite and predominantly masculine archetypes or grand acts of heroism. The word "bravery" conjures images of battlefield gallantry, overcoming inconceivable challenges, fighting fiery infernos, parachuting into enemy territory, intervening a robbery, or rescuing a drowning child. But that's not all bravery is.

Yes, there is "heroic" bravery in the face of extreme risk, but there is also "everyday" bravery in the face of smaller challenges. Too seldom do we perceive bravery as being something that most people encounter in everyday situations. How about questioning a process, giving feedback to an employee, or making an apology?

People have a marvelous ability to be oblivious or dismissive of the fact that they practice some form of bravery all the time. We assure ourselves that our actions are "no big deal" or "anyone would have done the same thing" without giving any accolades to the emotional processes or choices that lead up to the action. Take the Cowardly Lion from the classic film *The Wizard of Oz*, for example. He was so ashamed of his own fear, anxiety, and perceived cowardice that he was unable to see his own innate bravery. The Cowardly Lion believed that having fear made him inadequate. On his quest to see the Wizard for a cure for this inadequacy, he was completely blind to the number of brave deeds he executed along the way.

We deal with a variety of obstacles and numerous fears every day on our own yellow brick road. Most of the time we dismiss our ability to overcome these as not worthy of acknowledgement. But as Marianne Williamson asserted, *"Your playing small does not serve the world."* Whether it's social conditioning, comparing ourselves to others, setting our internal bar of what qualifies as courage too high, or lacking confidence, why are we afraid of referring to ourselves as brave? Why do we have a habit of mistaking the extraordinary for the ordinary?

Recognizing your own bravery, no matter how insignificant the situation might feel to you, is one of the most empowering things you can do. It ignites your confidence and personal effectiveness. If you don't consider yourself to be brave already or, at least, as having a strong capacity for bravery then you aren't giving yourself the credit you deserve. When you deny or dismiss the ways that you show bravery in your actions, it keeps you small and powerless.

Once you start to consider bravery in this way, it is easy to chart your own history of bravery. Quitting a job, getting married, buying a house, confronting a friend, facing your fear of heights, setting boundaries with a coworker... the list goes on. Any action that involved a bit of risk and some fear represents a form of bravery and you have certainly done many of them.

To develop a deeper appreciation for your own bravery, I suggest you try the following: keep a record of your daily bravery for two weeks. At the end of each day reflect on the times that you felt apprehensive, doubtful, or uneasy. Recall if those feelings stopped you from taking action or if you pushed forward despite the fear. At the end of the two weeks review the frequency with which you acted bravely.

Bravery is like a muscle that needs conditioning, discipline, and plenty of opportunities for practice. It takes time to develop bravery so don't be too dismissive of your efforts. Keep asking yourself, "How big is my brave today?" Be proactive with bravery, look for opportunities where you can practice being one degree braver than you were the time before.

One strategy that I frequently engage in for taking everyday brave action is Mel Robbins' Five Second Rule. The idea is simple. When faced with a decision or an instinct to act on something, especially if it causes you to hesitate, don't allow your mind enough time to talk you out of the right action or take the easier path. Your mind is an excellent negotiator and advocate for backing down. Silence it. Take a deep breath, count down from five to one, then act.

THE SIX FACES OF BRAVERY

Adapted from the blog Lion's Whiskers by Dr. Lisa Dungate, PsyD and Jennifer Armstrong, here are six ways to categorize and develop bravery (what I call "The Six Faces of Bravery") to help us navigate life's challenges: Physical, Social, Moral, Emotional, Intellectual, and Spiritual.

THE FACE OF PHYSICAL BRAVERY

"A single feat of daring can alter the whole conception of what is possible."
— **Graham Greene**

Physical is the most apparent type of bravery as it can involve choosing to act despite the risk of bodily harm, suffering, or death. Developing physical bravery can include increasing physical strength, improving overall physical health, building stamina, resilience, and alertness.

Some examples that might come to mind first of physical bravery include a soldier in combat, fending off an attacker, jumping out of an airplane, fighting a fire, rescuing someone in trouble, or performing a risky medical procedure. But unless you are repeatedly in perilous situations, such as a high-risk occupation, these instances will be uncommon.

However, there are many other types of physical bravery that do not carry a risk of actual physical harm, but rather the risk of perceived harm – or physical fear. Physical fear is usually wildly disproportionate: our minds construct that the challenge we are facing is much more precarious than it actually is and it's the apprehension we feel that stops us from taking action. That foreboding can be debilitating, especially if we are drawing on a previous experience that had a negative outcome, but often our fear is just a barrier that we need to cross to go beyond our comfort zone and into an area that allows us to grow.

Physical bravery also includes the awareness that your physical health is what prepares you to engage with the world and what condition you choose to keep your body in can make a tremendous difference in how equipped you are to manage other demands.

The face of physical bravery looks like:

- Getting back on the bike after you fell off
- Walking into the gym when you feel too unfit to be there
- Training for a marathon (or any competitive sporting event)
- Committing to a healthy eating plan
- Wearing a bathing suit
- Signing up for a program or class that intimidates you
- Trying a food that you've never tried before
- Getting regular medical and dental exams
- Undergoing an operation or medical procedure
- Being sexually intimate

THE FACE OF SOCIAL BRAVERY

"Courage is what it takes to stand up and speak; courage is also what it takes to sit down and listen."
— **Winston Churchill**

Social bravery is having integrity, holding your head high, and feeling comfortable in your own skin – even at the risk of social humiliation, unpopularity, or rejection. Social bravery means not conforming to the expectations of others. It's being authentically you, even if the result is social disapproval. It is not about seeking attention; it's about tolerating attention. It's about asking for what you want or need.

It's also about treating people in the way *they* wish to be treated rather than the way you wish to be treated. It's about apologizing and moving on. It's standing up for the person being bullied at school or in the workplace. It's loving your quirky differences. It means expressing your ideas, opinions, or preferences even if they are not "in line" with everyone else's ideas, opinions, or preferences.

Social bravery is seen in emotionally intelligent leadership, not in top-down management. It's about driving positive change in the organization. It's actively engaging in diversity efforts. It's welcoming ideas that are different from your own. It's risking being perceived as a "Sensitive New Age Guy" to promote gender equality. It's about leading with your values. It's about being okay with resistance.

The face of social bravery looks like:

- Having a personal fashion style
- Coming out with your sexual orientation
- Disclosing a mental health condition

- Delivering a presentation with confidence
- Giving or receiving feedback
- Disagreeing with someone
- Being graceful about rejection
- Setting boundaries
- Addressing conflict/having difficult conversations
- Keeping your word
- Standing up for yourself

THE FACE OF INTELLECTUAL BRAVERY

"It is impossible for a man to learn what he
thinks he already knows."

— Epictetus

Intellectual bravery is a willingness to engage with complex ideas, to question our assumptions, and to risk being wrong. It means being able to think critically, ask questions, and challenge opposing beliefs or data. It's exploring new information with an open mind when what we learn contradicts the beliefs or teachings from a family, culture, or religious group.

It's about checking the source before you accept what you hear or read as truth. It's admitting when you don't know the answer or speaking up if you are struggling to gain understanding. It's accepting the presence of bias in our thinking and training yourself to see yours and move beyond it. It's understanding the difference between what is subjective and what is objective.

Given our easy and indiscriminate access to the explosion of information in recent decades, it has become vitally important to be an intellectually brave critical thinker instead of a passive recipient of information. Intellectual bravery will be an increasingly required skill in the future, as complex structural problems of the environment, economy, and society challenge conventional problem-solving.

The face of intellectual bravery looks like:

- Asking questions
- Listening to other people's questions
- Learning a new skill
- Being slower to judge or criticize
- Understanding your own strengths and limitations
- Questioning how it's "always been done"
- Seeking out opposing points of view
- Admitting mistakes
- Questioning "facts" or news
- Testing different hypotheses before drawing conclusions

THE FACE OF MORAL BRAVERY

"Stand up for what is right even if you stand alone."
— Suzy Kassem

Moral bravery means doing the right thing even at the risk of inconvenience, opposition, disapproval, or loss of security. It involves ethics and integrity, a decision to match our words and actions with our values and ideals. It means listening to our conscience: that quiet voice within that wants to guide you.

To be morally brave requires us to discern what actions or behaviors are supportive of our highest ideals and which ones are damaging. It asks us to recognize our responsibilities and see the potential consequences of our own actions. It also involves the courage to resist personal gain at the expense of others.

It's about confronting ethical dilemmas and taking action when the easier thing to do would be to turn a blind eye. It can involve challenging others who are behaving inappropriately at the risk of being tarred with the same brush as those committing less than savory practices. Moral bravery could mean pointing out gender, sexuality, or race issues that have become commonly accepted practices in a workplace and taking a stand against it. It's beginning a movement to abolish outdated and unfair practices.

Moral bravery also challenges us to rise above the apathy, complacency, contempt, prejudice, and fear-mongering in our political systems, socioeconomic divisions, and cultural/religious differences.

The face of moral bravery looks like:

- Helping someone who's having trouble, even if it's inconvenient for you
- Picking up litter
- Acting with integrity when no one's looking
- Turning in a lost wallet
- Giving all people an equal voice regardless of race, socioeconomic status, religion, gender, or sexual orientation
- A company whistleblower risking job loss, financial cost, and/or legal repercussion
- Reporting a crime
- Handing money back to a cashier if you received too much change
- Boycotting products from an unethical company

THE FACE OF EMOTIONAL BRAVERY

"Courage means feeling all those hard human emotions – all that uncertainty and anxiety – and getting the job done anyway."
— Douglas Conant

Emotional bravery is being willing to be aware of, and vulnerable to, the full spectrum of positive and negative emotions. It's the driving force behind anything genuine that we do. When we choose to ignore, suppress, or deny our emotion, we risk a reduction of insight, which can lead to faulty decisions, damaged relationships, poor performance, and disengaged behavior.

Emotional bravery asks us to manage our emotions so that we are able to control our responses. It's about ensuring that we express the right feeling, to the right person, to the right degree, at the right time. It's being strategic and intentional with expressing feelings to achieve desirable outcomes. To be emotionally brave also allows us to be confident, connected, consistent, and committed. Those four elements are essential ingredients for outstanding leadership.

Emotional bravery also means loving yourself, being proud of yourself, and believing that you are worthy of love and happiness. Emotional bravery is a critical tool to use as you navigate your road to self-mastery. Emotional bravery can fill you with confidence to move outside your comfort zone and explore the unfamiliar, where growth happens.

The face of emotional bravery looks like:

- Being genuinely happy for someone else's success
- Being present for someone who is feeling strong emotions
- Forgiving someone you love
- Forgiving yourself

- Expressing gratitude
- Expressing appropriate emotions in a workplace
- Crying without embarrassment or apology
- Helping a stranger who is in distress
- Engaging in self-reflection
- Spending time alone

THE FACE OF SPIRITUAL BRAVERY

"This is my simple religion. There is no need for temples; no need for complicated philosophy. Our own brain, our own heart is our temple; the philosophy is kindness."
— His Holiness the Dalai Lama

Spiritual bravery entails asking questions about faith, purpose, and meaning – either in a religious or nonreligious framework. Many people find strength in an organized religion, but there are many other ways to develop spiritual bravery.

Spiritual bravery means having an open and willing mind to ask the deepest questions about why we are here and what our purpose is. It involves accepting that you are unlikely to find concrete answers and being comfortable with uncertainty. It also might involve letting go of a strongly held belief and accepting that there might be other beliefs that are as valid as your own.

Spiritual bravery means opening ourselves up to our own vulnerability, mortality, and the mysteries of life and death. It means being compassionate and understanding about the different beliefs people have regarding appropriate rituals and choices for death and dying, as well as traditions for grieving. It also involves being open and honest with children about death.

Spiritual bravery allows us to engage with people of different religious faiths and spiritual traditions without judgment. It allows us to cultivate respect for others, their beliefs, and their culture. It can also include forming friendships with people from faith traditions other than your own.

The face of spiritual bravery looks like:

- Making time to pray, meditate, or do charitable work
- Letting go of the need to control everything in life
- Appreciating the beauty and complexity of nature
- Building meaningful rituals into your daily life
- Learning a bit about the Koran, the Bible, Talmudic teachings, Buddhist teachings, etc.
- Attending a religious celebration outside of your own belief system
- Accepting that spirituality can exist outside the walls of a religious institution
- Writing a will
- Taking out a life insurance policy

WHAT DOES YOUR FACE OF BRAVERY LOOK LIKE?

"Fear is a reaction. Courage is a decision."
— Winston Churchill

In any of its faces, bravery is a decision. It's a decision to take a stand and fight when appropriate rather than run or turn a blind eye. To be inquisitive instead of dogmatic. To persevere rather than give up. To act with integrity rather than deceit. To accept responsibility rather than blame. To seek information rather than preach. To strive for constant improvement rather than regress or stagnate. To build rather than destroy. To love rather than hate. To lean into our own greatness rather than shrink away from it. To confront one's own shadow rather than ignoring its presence. To consciously face the existential facts of suffering, infirmity, and death rather than denying them.

Bravery is a skill which allows us to overcome our inhibitions, our real or imagined fears, and gives us the strength to do what we feel is right, despite the risks involved. It is something which promotes in us a sense of self-belief which can cause us to scale mountains and do things which we never believed we could. Bravery doesn't come from what you're already confident you can do; it comes from triumphing over things you once thought you couldn't.

A person's willingness to be brave is a prime determinant of how successful they will be in their life. No matter how you choose to define success, bravery will be an underpinning competency that precedes the victory. Our level of bravery also determines how we feel about ourselves, too. I have never heard of a person who practiced cowardice and had a genuinely high sense of self-worth.

To be BADASS every day, we must be consciously and consistently practicing bravery in all that we do. Small steps are perfect. Perhaps the bravest step that you can take right now is to decide to lean into your most powerful self (whatever that currently looks and feels like) and allow yourself to become more confident and self-assured. The majority of people are more afraid of being powerful than of being powerless. Powerlessness is easy – all you have to do is blame, deflect, ignore, and condemn – and you can remain effectively powerless for all the days of your life. Being powerful takes bravery and true ownership.

If you feel you are already skillfully practicing bravery, that's fantastic! *How can you be doing it even better? Is there another area of your life where you apply a touch more bravery? How about activating a different type of bravery that you have less experience with?* Do things every day that are difficult and continue to rise. Your most powerful self does not have a ceiling.

There will always be risks, there will always be naysayers, there will always be adversity of some kind to face – those things are guaranteed. As you travel down your road to self-mastery you will hit bumps that will discourage you from taking brave action. Bumps are okay; they only jolt you temporarily. Just don't allow yourself to get stuck in a rut where you are not moving forward at all. Embrace the obstacles that push you and show you who you really are.

And as the sun rises and you greet each new day, ask yourself, "How big is my brave today?"

CHAPTER SIX

WHO ARE YOU? (AUTHENTIC)

"Authenticity is a collection of choices that we have to make every day. It's about the choice to show up and be real. The choice to be honest. The choice to let our true selves be seen."

— Brené Brown

O ur second piece of the BADASS framework focuses on arguably the most important question you can ever ask, and answer, yourself: "Who am I?" Exploring your authentic self can be really hard work. It requires awareness, commitment, bravery, vulnerability, and patience. But it pays off in a multitude of intrapersonal and interpersonal ways. When we choose to be authentic, we invite people into our lives who hold authenticity and truth in high regard, as well.

Badasses are virtuous individuals who don't just "talk the talk," they also "walk the walk." That means they uphold their commitments and back up their impactful words with consistent actions that benefit themselves and others. Do what you say you're going to do. Lance Secretan remarked, *"Authenticity is the alignment of head, mouth, heart, and feet – thinking, saying, feeling, and doing the same thing – consistently."*

Genuinely authentic people tend to be fully accepting of themselves and others, own their mistakes and seek to understand the lessons, are able to express their emotions clearly, and understand what drives them. To behave authentically, we must first give deep thought to what is important to us, how we want to show up, and how we want to influence those around us. Get to know yourself better than you currently do. Be mindful of your emotions. Observe how your emotions affect your choices and decisions. Be on alert to how your actions impact others. Act in accordance with your values and you'll generate trust and be noted for your authenticity.

THE LABELS WE WEAR

Can you remember who you were before other people told you who you should be?

We are trained from birth to see ourselves as others define us. We are given a name by our parents and we never question it or change it; we simply wear that name for the rest of our lives. As we progress through traditional education systems, we are categorized by our perceived skills, abilities, and observable behaviors. Standardized testing models tell us what our strengths and weaknesses are. We begin to form our identity around what other people or systems say we are good, or bad, at. We etch those labels in concrete in our minds and design our lives and our futures around them.

As we mature, we are taught to act in a principled and honorable way, to know our place, to not cause problems, to do what you're told, conform, and only have as much power or influence as other people think you should have. If we reject the unspoken rules of mainstream society, bravely attempt to step outside the walls of conformity to follow our heart, and we misstep, we can be shamed into identifying with our failure – sometimes by the people that care about us the most. Rather than embracing our creativity, courage, and learnings, we learn to fear effort and risk. We feel haunted by our mistakes, so we dedicate our energy to regret.

We are taught by examples of behavior we see reported on in the media to blame others and shirk responsibility for our actions or choices. When we model that behavior in our own life, we start to see ourselves as passive and helpless and become incapable of embracing accountability or forgiveness, for ourselves or for others.

Our Western culture places high value on individualism and teaches us to focus on our differences, not on our similarities – to see people as less than or better than ourselves. We pin our self-worth to where we think we sit in the hierarchy we create in our minds, while condemning the differences of those above and below us.

As we go through our lives, more labels get attached to us from the things we accumulate – degrees, marriages, kids, divorces, career choices, resumes, income, assets, net worth, philanthropy, physical appearance – and we mistake these brandings as our core identity, our essence. We use these labels as measuring sticks to determine our value, our purpose, and our contribution to this world. As a consequence, we forget who we really are, if we ever knew in the first place.

WILL THE REAL YOU PLEASE STAND UP?

"Authenticity is the daily practice of letting go of who we think we're supposed to be and embracing who we are."

— **Brené Brown**

The reason *"Who are you?"* is perhaps the most challenging question a person could ever be called to answer is because most of us already think we have a crystal clear perception of our identity. The truth is, we are often blinded by the lies we tell ourselves about who we are and how we want others to see us. Most people are completely unaware that they feed themselves these lies and don't actually know their own truth. We also internalize other people's perceptions of us and that forms the foundation for our reality. Allow me to describe an example of this.

There was a well-respected university professor who had an incredibly accomplished academic career. A prolific writer and researcher, he was frequently published in academic journals and sought after to speak at other universities, often drawing large crowds of students and faculty to hear what he had to say. He was frequently told how much he was admired in his field and was referred to as a pioneer, a genius, and a master. Over time, his career and the perceptions of him from those in the academic world became the foundation that he built his identity on. One Christmas Eve, the professor's wife and only child were killed in an automobile accident. Heartbroken, the grieving professor took a six-month sabbatical and travelled to Cambodia, his late wife's home country, to lay his family's ashes to rest in her hometown. He stayed in Cambodia for four years.

Why did he remain overseas for so long? What happened was that the professor realized that in Cambodia nobody knew about his illustrious academic achievements, nor did they really care. Most of the people in his wife's village didn't even know what a professor was. When he would try to explain it, they demonstrated their understanding by nodding and pointing to the one-room shack that was used to teach the village children. In that village he had no title, no clout – in fact, most of the villagers didn't even use his name. They called him "barang" which means a "foreigner, particularly of European ancestry" in the Khmer language.

Unable to hide behind the academic armor he had built over several decades, the professor became aware that he had no idea who he was without it. Further, without his labels as a husband and a father, he had no connection with his authentic self, period. He had let his job, his family, and his reputation define him. The professor vowed to remain in Cambodia for as long as it took to discover his true core identity.

THE THREE LIES

This story illustrates the three lies, according to Henri Nouwen, that most people tell themselves about their identity: *I am what I have. I am what I do. I am what other people say or think about me.*

It's completely normal to question who you are or what's important to you, especially since we change so much throughout our lives. We go through many phases over the course of an average lifetime: we change relationships, careers, we have children, and sometimes we experience tragedy or loss that jolts us into asking big questions or reevaluating priorities. Over time, your major life events and influences may prompt you to question your values, your spiritual beliefs, your interests, your career path, or how you see yourself.

But left unchecked, those three lies can also deceive you into identifying with all the things you lack, that you don't do, and the unkind things that people have said or thought about you.

CORE VALUES: LET'S GET PERSONAL

What is most important to you? Your core values determine how you answer this question. Your core values guide your behavior, providing you with a personal code of conduct. They highlight your standards and represent the essence of you. There is tremendous power in values. Your core values will serve as your soul's compass as you navigate your road to self-mastery.

When people live by their values, they experience greater connection to their authentic self, which leads to increased fulfillment and happiness. When people don't honor their values, they create internal conflict and their mental, emotional, and physical health suffers. The problem is, most people don't know what their core values are or what's important to them. Or worse, they do know and consciously choose to ignore them. Instead, we put priority and focus on what our society, culture, and media tell us to value.

I buy essential oils from a small-business owner in New South Wales named Kim. Kim has a notably personal touch with all of her customers that attracted me from the first time I placed an order with her shop, Feather & Seed. Her authenticity is extraordinary and is one of the reasons I will continue to buy from her and recommend her business to others. Kim recently sent an email to her client base apologizing for not replying to the people who had left a product review on her site over the previous two years and promising a response in the coming days. She explained that when she added review software to her store, she listened to the advice of marketing professionals who insisted it is best to *not* comment on reviews unless it is a direct question. For two years, Kim felt rude and ungrateful and it caused her torment because she was acting out of alignment with her core values.

Impressed, I reached out to Kim to applaud her for listening to her heart. She responded, "It can be so easy to lose yourself in business and stray off the path. It seems our values and ethics are layered with 'what we should be doing' rather than what we actually feel. I remember my Buddhist teacher telling me years ago that if you do not fully believe in something, research it, and if it still does not sit well with you then chuck it out. I find that easier to do in my personal life, but harder in business. I was so relieved to send that email."

WHAT ARE YOUR CORE VALUES?

"If someone isn't what others want them to be, the others become angry. Everyone seems to have a clear idea of how other people should lead their lives, but none about his or her own."

— Paulo Coelho, *The Alchemist*

Can you name your core values off the top of your head? Unless you have gone through a discovery process or actively prioritize awareness of your core values, it's challenging to readily identify what is important to you. It's easy to get confused with what you think you should value because you have many streams of input coming at you from all directions telling you different things – your family, your religion, your profession, your friends, the media, etc. Tuning out the white noise and leaning in to who you authentically are and what your unique core values are takes a lot of effort.

A Values Discovery Process should ideally be done with a qualified coach to guide you, but you can do it yourself as long as you are rigorously honest with yourself about your answers. One way that I do this discovery process is to review a list of common core values (Check out my Core Values List: https://www.nikkilangman.

com/post/core-values). Then, write down ALL of the values that resonate with you – select as many as you want. You don't need to restrict yourself to what is on the list, either. A list primarily serves as a prompt to get your ideas churning. Once you have done that, take a highlighter to the list you just made and select ten that are the most important to you. With a different highlighter, narrow that ten down to your top three to five. These are your core values. Remember: this is a DIY exercise so treat it as a rough draft, but it should give you indicators of the things you personally put the most value on. Over time, clarity will emerge.

Ask yourself questions as you are selecting what you feel is important to you so that you are focusing on your authentic self, not your desired self-image. What commendations have you received that are the most meaningful to you? How does it make you feel when you are complimented on your appearance, your quality of work, your parenting skills, or the way you show up for others? All endorsements are nice, but a few will stand out for you. Explore those.

Conversely, what makes you really angry – like, blood boiling angry? How do you respond differently to some offenses? I am a vocally expressive person. When I get mad, my volume goes up and I verbally attack. When one of my values has been violated, I go silent and retreat into myself. I joke with my family, "If I yell, I'll get over it; if I get quiet, worry." I am acutely aware of the difference between an irritation and something that cuts to my core.

Your core values should be your blueprint for your behaviors, decisions, and actions. When you know what you value, you can align your choices accordingly. The last step is to put your core values in a place(s) where they are visible to you daily. Sticky notes, reminder apps, and screen savers are great for this. My core values are bravery, integrity, grit, and humor. I wear a necklace that has those four words etched onto interlinked rings, so my core values are literally next to my heart every day. You will also find them displayed on my website and on many of my business communications. Grit is the core value that I lean on when I race, so before every race I take a permanent marker and write that word on the back of my hand. Your core values are a huge part of your authentic self so live and breathe them in everything you do.

Over your lifetime there will be thousands of things that are important to you and that you will value, so remember it this way: everything that's important to you can be written in your biography. Your core values are what you want written on your tombstone.

THE GUY IN THE GLASS

The Guy in the Glass has been one of my favorite poems since I was a teenager. There have been many variations of this work with increasingly modern language over the years, but the message about being true to yourself is timeless. I chose to use the original version here because it made sense to me to credit the authentic words for a poem written about authenticity.

THE GUY IN THE GLASS
by Dale Wimbrow, (c) 1934

When you get what you want in your struggle for pelf,
And the world makes you King for a day,
Then go to the mirror and look at yourself,
And see what that guy has to say.

For it isn't your Father, or Mother, or Wife,
Who judgment upon you must pass.
The feller whose verdict counts most in your life
Is the guy staring back from the glass.

He's the feller to please, never mind all the rest,
For he's with you clear up to the end,
And you've passed your most dangerous, difficult test
If the guy in the glass is your friend.

You may be like Jack Horner and "chisel" a plum,
And think you're a wonderful guy,
But the man in the glass says you're only a bum
If you can't look him straight in the eye.

You can fool the whole world down the pathway of years,
And get pats on the back as you pass,
But your final reward will be heartaches and tears
If you've cheated the guy in the glass.

To this day, the message shakes my heart. We will only ever be content if we are living in alignment with our core values. Living outside of our values is like wearing someone else's wet bathing suit. However, even if we are clear on what is internally important, most of us do behave in ways that are inauthentic from time to time. In some situations, we can place emphasis on impressing or pleasing others, being liked or accepted, or avoiding conflict, so much so that we choose to behave in a way that doesn't feel right. If we do this too often, we start to chip away at and lose touch with our authentic self.

It's important to recognize that this is a natural part of being human and navigating relationships. Not everyone is going to think the same way you do and share your same values, so sometimes we don't even perceive that something feels off to us until we are already deep in a situation. What becomes critical is to develop the self-awareness to notice when you have that wet bathing suit feeling and correct your behavior to get into alignment with your core values as soon as you observe what is happening.

I used to feel like I had to give everyone my resume in order to feel worthy of praise. I convinced myself that if I put the spotlight on all of the things about me that were admirable and impressive then I could hide my ugly parts in the shadows and no one would notice. But the truth is that applause only lasts for so long and what you have left after recognition and attention die down are your own thoughts and perceptions about yourself. *Are your behaviors worthy of your own applause?*

WHERE IS YOUR QUERENCIA?

Querencia is an abstract idea in the Spanish language that stems from the Spanish verb "querer," meaning "to want or desire." Modern translations explain querencia as the place where one's strength of character is drawn, where one feels secure; the place where you are your most authentic self.

Ascribed to bullfighting, querencia is the place in the ring the wounded bull will instinctively gravitate toward to renew his strength, where he feels most solid and powerful.

Ernest Hemingway's book, *Death in the Afternoon*, explains querencia like this:

"A querencia is a place the bull naturally wants to go to in the ring, a preferred locality... It is a place which develops in the course of the fight where the bull makes his home. It does not usually show at once, but develops in his brain as the fight goes on. In this place he feels that he has his back against the wall and in his querencia he is inestimably more dangerous and almost impossible to kill."

— Ernest Hemingway, *Death in the Afternoon*

The matador attunes himself to the bull's movements and tries to keep him away from this place, because it decreases the bull's vulnerability. The matador retains the advantage as long as the bull is disoriented. It is thought that if the same bull were to fight more than once in the same ring, he would kill the matador every time; once the bull learns the game and stands in his power, he cannot be conquered.

Other animals have intuitive querencia for the purpose of survival. Some are masters of camouflage, some burrow into rock or sand, construct complex caves, migrate to the exact location year after year, hunt in the dark or during storms when they're less likely to be detected, or know to make haste toward a creek line when confronted by a fire.

Humans have querencia, too. Our querencia can be a physical location, a ritual, a behavior, or something else that reconnects us with our center and helps us feel most secure and renewed. The answers are inside us, should we choose to listen. Some people can easily identify what helps them feel grounded: it might be a pull toward fresh mountain air or watching ocean waves crash, or another connection with nature – walking in a park or breathing in the aroma of flowers. Some feel peaceful in a certain location inside their home, wearing clothes of a particular style, smelling freshly brewed coffee, listening to specific music, or engaging in a favorite activity or sport.

I feel in my querencia in bustling cities. I thrive on the commotion, the competing smells of fast food, the graffiti, and the drone of honking cars and sirens. I love the challenge of fighting oncoming pedestrians and feeling like a salmon swimming upstream. I feel empowered listening to Hare Krishnas' chant mantras and dance down crowded streets and I often pause, enthralled, to watch buskers and marvel at street performers. The chaos of the city calms me and I feel sharp, focused, and grounded. I choose to live in a high-rise apartment and when I need quiet contemplative time, I stand on my balcony and allow myself to be mesmerized by the twinkling city lights. I run alone in busy public spaces, like city parks and heavily-trafficked bicycle and pedestrian routes. "Alone in a crowd" is my happy place and being in that space makes me feel strong and powerful, with a renewed spirit and positive emotional energy.

An intense environment like a swarming city may not appeal to you at all. Good. Cross that off your list for now. Sometimes the most effective way to understand your querencia is to go through a process of elimination. Think about different activities and environments and ask yourself if they invite you or not.

There are times where I cannot be in my element and I notice the difference. I can easily feel agitated, overwhelmed, and vulnerable to stressors. Like the matador, those irritants can push me around, affect my behavior, and hold me at a disadvantage. At these times I have to tap into one of my other substitute querencias that are more accessible in that moment. It's important to have a few options of places you can go, rituals you can practice, or activities you can engage in that give you that sense of strength and safety.

Do you ever feel like the disoriented and exposed bull in the ring, aware of the dangers that surround you, but choked by fear and unable to gain any kind of control or clarity? Humans tend to overthink and overcommit to external things and therefore ignore or minimize their instincts and needs. This is where we need to engage the skills of self-awareness and self-management to help us understand and manage the chatter around us and mindfully explore ourselves further.

Search for your querencia. You'll identify it. It might take a bit of persistence for the answers to reveal themselves, but they are there, inside of you. Keep asking yourself and visualizing: Where do you come from? Where do you feel most alive? What happens to you in that place? What feelings do you experience there? Are you alone, or with someone else? What are you doing?

Once you have some clear ideas, surround yourself with those reminders. Find photographs of you in that location, or with those people, or doing that activity. Maybe you have tangible objects like trophies, souvenirs, plants, or gifts that bring you back to your querencia. Whatever it is, treat it like your charger. Keep it close and when your batteries run low, plug into that source of strength to renew and refill your energy.

THE LIFE YOU ARE TRULY HERE TO LIVE

Perhaps the biggest hurdle to living more authentically is that in order to connect with our truth we must first confront our discontentment. It means getting honest about the lies that we have supported ourselves with for so long. It means forgiving ourselves for abandoning our own needs and allowing the world to make us do fear's bidding. It means accepting that once we reveal what's behind the mask, we will never be able to ignorantly put it back on and pretend that we don't know who we are. Being authentic is about being brave enough to define our own version of success and pursue that path with our whole heart. As soon as we limit ourselves, we might get accolades and achieve other people's interpretation of success, but we risk letting fulfillment slip from our grasp.

Australian author Bronnie Ware wrote a book in 2012 inspired by her work as a palliative carer called, *The Top Five Regrets of the Dying*. In it, she asks patients on their deathbeds, at the time where they can perhaps most clearly see the value of life, about their greatest regrets. Their number one regret: *"I wish I'd had the courage to live a life true to myself, not the life others expected of me."*

Be bold. Be **BADASS** every day. Be courageous enough to authentically live the life you are truly here to live.

CHAPTER SEVEN

FOLLOW YOUR NORTH STAR (DIRECTION)

"The mystery of human existence lies not in just staying alive, but in finding something to live for."

— **Fyodor Dostoevsky**

Traditionally, during journeys of the past when navigation science was primitive, navigators of the land or sea would carve out the path for their journey by looking in the direction of the North Star for guidance (assuming they were in the Northern Hemisphere). According to astronomers, the North Star (aka Polaris) is famous for holding nearly still, only tracing a tiny arc in our sky while the entire northern sky moves around it.

This brings us to our third component of the BADASS framework: Direction. To be your most powerful badass self every day, you need to be clear on what direction you are going in and why. You need to follow your own North Star. Metaphorically, your North Star is your vision, your direction, and your purpose. It's a steady destination or goal that you can always look toward for guidance as the world changes around you. When you aren't confident about what direction you are headed, you are lost, stagnant, or worse – going down a path that's not serving you.

Following your North Star helps you live with purpose and gives you a reference point to keep you moving in the right direction. Having purpose doesn't prevent life from being challenging. Discouragement and obstacles will always present themselves. But when you're living with purpose, it grounds you and makes it much easier to stay on track and resilient to the storms that come your way.

UNDERSTANDING PURPOSE

Purpose is an age-old topic that has been pondered throughout history by many philosophers and theologians, and by pretty much everyone at one point or another. In today's fast-paced, technology-driven world where we are being pulled in many directions at once, identifying your purpose is more important than ever.

Life has a way of keeping us distracted and focused only on chores and problem-solving. Day after day and week after week, many people go about their work and their daily lives without much consideration of anything else. They spend their days reacting to situations and being controlled by the events that happen around them instead of being proactive and anchoring their choices and actions to meaning and values. But we are created to do so much more than simply exist and go through the motions; we are designed to thrive and build a life that we love, not just make a living or overcome hurdles.

YOUR PERSONAL LEGEND

One of my favorite ways to describe purpose is as a "Personal Legend" from the book *The Alchemist* by Paulo Coelho. A Personal Legend is one's destiny in life. When the main character, Santiago, meets an old King he teaches the boy what a Personal Legend is. The King explains that a Personal Legend is "what you have always wanted to accomplish." It's an ultimate goal that you have for your life that's driven forward by possibility, not fear. You follow this path because it has an intention, it serves a desire, and it helps you live with purpose. This means living up to your highest potential as the extraordinary human being you are. Naturally, you might need to develop particular skills and strengths in certain areas of your life, but that's all part of the work involved in fulfilling your Personal Legend.

GOALS AND PASSIONS

> *"Determine what you want and why you want it. Once you understand what's important, you can utilize your passions and achieve anything."*
> — **Brooke Griffin**

People often confuse purpose with short-term goals or passions. Goals and passions are the "what:" they are the things that you love to do that keep your tank full of energy and in motion. They can be all over the place, untamed and stimulating, and create a lot of variety in your life.

Whereas purpose is steadier and more directed: it's your "why," your longer-term objectives. Goals and passions are more inwardly-focused; they are your way of measuring progress. Purpose is outwardly-focused; it is the impact you have on others and your environment. Purpose can also be much more encompassing since, when you look up at your night sky, you will always see it in front of you – guiding you – but it's not a precise road map of how to get from A to B.

PURPOSE IS FLUID

Do you ever feel pressured, like you should have a massive and clear plan for your entire existence, and you don't? I have liberating news for you: you don't need to. Your purpose is fluid and likely to develop and change shape as you grow and evolve. You may have a significant life experience that pushes you in a different direction than the one you thought you were headed in. Sometimes events will happen outside of your control that can cause you to shift course and make adjustments to your purpose. You might also reach your current destination, which means it's time to reset your compass. This could mean an extension of your current direction or a new one altogether. It's okay for your North Star to transform over time. But whatever it is right now, let it guide you. Day after day, we are always headed in one direction or another. As the days add up, it becomes the path, for better or worse, of a person's life.

A few people seem to have incredibly clear visions and life purpose right from a young age, but most do not. Some people have several North Stars, which is perfectly fine as long as they are moving in the same direction so there is no conflict among them. And sometimes a person has a single North Star, one objective, one philosophy, that draws together all the dimensions of his or her life. The beauty of fluidity is that you retain power over your purpose at all times by understanding its dynamic nature and your ability to reframe your purpose whenever you need to.

WHY DO MOST PEOPLE NOT HAVE PURPOSE?

For amusement, I sometimes entertain the visual that our society strongly resembles The Walking Dead, with a herd of directionless bodies lumbering around, going about monotonous daily activity, without any destination. As much as I like zombies, they are not badasses.

There are many individual reasons why a person might be navigating through life without any clear direction, but my experience and research have revealed that the majority of people are either struggling to define their purpose but would love to get there, or they have wrestled with it at some point and given up trying to clarify it. Here's some suggestions from Shelley Prevost as to why people grapple with purpose:

1. They didn't have effective guidance.
2. They're checking the boxes.
3. They don't like the dark side of themselves.
4. They don't value the unconscious life.

Let's inspect these in more detail.

THEY DIDN'T HAVE EFFECTIVE GUIDANCE

People are trained to look to others for leadership and instruction from a tender age. We are taught how to act, how to behave, how to consider options, and create strategies, but the trouble starts when that coaching crosses over into something as personal as your life or career choices.

For some people, this guidance worked and with the assistance of a parent, teacher, coach, or other leader they identified their unique purpose. If that sounds like your story, you are truly fortunate.

But most people, even with the most well-meaning advisors, are fit into a box that makes sense to the advisor. Because we have been coached to trust our advisors and we want to please them, we willingly slide into that box. Even if the box doesn't feel right, we will more readily change ourselves to better fit the box than change the box to better fit ourselves. Little by little we reject our true selves and lose touch with what's genuinely important to us. Too often, we play the starring role in a script that someone else wrote.

THEY'RE CHECKING THE BOXES

Our culture has dictated a list of what acceptable forms of success are and, the more boxes you can check, the more successful you are perceived to be: graduate from a reputable school, get married, create a family, establish yourself in a low- to medium-risk career path, accumulate enough wealth for a few assets and an annual vacation, build a retirement portfolio, and maintain job and family security.

This tried-and-true roadmap is fantastic for promoting conformity, but not at all ideal for identifying and following our unique purpose. Even if we can admit to ourselves that we aren't fulfilled with those definitions of success, too often we cling to our illusions because they're all we know. So, we make choices because they match the boxes we've been directed to check.

We're so busy tending to our monotonous to-do list that we rarely stop and consider, "Am I content and satisfied? And if not, how should I start to make some changes?" If you have ever asked yourself "Is this all there is?" then it's probably worth your time to explore that thought further.

Purpose is passionate and persistent. It starts as a curiosity ("I wonder what would happen if…") and then takes on a life of its own with confident and dogged determination.

Following your North Star isn't an easy path, which is why most of us never seek it out. Many people fear that the path they've chosen isn't the right one, or feel resistance from those who would prefer that they travel the paved roads. We fear the risk, the potential missteps, the judgment, and the unknown. This uncertainty can easily knock someone off-course and lead to abandonment of their desires. This is especially perilous if your chosen path bears no fruit for a while before you begin to see results, such as entrepreneurship.

Your purpose might have nothing to do with what you currently do for work. Maybe your purpose right now is more about navigating a journey of self-discovery. Sometimes that process can take a great deal of soul-searching and time. Oftentimes, our career path will naturally take a different shape once we become clear on where our interests lie and what's important to us.

THEY DON'T LIKE THE DARK SIDE OF THEMSELVES

Remember the deep part of the well I talked about in Chapter Four: Oh, the Places You'll Go! where the nasties hang out such as your fears, repressed emotions, doubts, limiting beliefs, shame, and regrets? Carl Jung called it the shadow, the unconscious side of your personality that you'd rather hide from others.

Many interpretations depict the shadow as negative, but "unfamiliar" is probably a better word. We tend to fear the unknown so it makes sense that the shadow side of ourselves gets unfavorably categorized. However, our dark side holds both our deepest insecurities as well as our unrealized potential. If we allow ourselves to see our shadow as "untapped" we can approach it with curiosity instead of disdain.

The ego, our conscious self that we readily share with the world, has the least to teach us about our purpose because it is carefully constructed and edited to reflect our desired self-image. We tend to seek out relationships that validate what we want people to see. Some people go to great lengths to maintain focus on their public ego, avoid the shadow altogether, and end up completely missing out on the intrinsic capabilities and talents stored there.

Your shadow holds the answers to your purpose. If discovering your purpose is really about a journey of self-discovery, your richest soil for growth is stored in your vulnerable darkness.

THEY DON'T VALUE THE UNCONSCIOUS LIFE

Referring to the well again, the second level of your well is your unconscious life – your dreams, beliefs, intuitions, your suppressed memories, your values, and core identity. Our culture tends to downplay the value of anything that is intangible or subjective.

To discover your purpose, you must get comfortable with exploring the emotional mind. You must accept ambiguity and become okay with not having clear-cut answers. You must allow yourself to feel and not try to overpower your feelings with rationalizations. Reasoning your way to a purposeful life usually doesn't work. This proposal is confronting for some people and they don't choose to go there, or worse, they don't think they need to. Which is why some people will live their entire lives never recognizing their true purpose.

HOW DO I FOLLOW MY NORTH STAR?

A lot of people truly want to be guided by their North Star but have no idea where to start. If you feel like you're lacking meaning in your life, it can be an unsettling feeling. You may feel frustrated and confused, and perhaps get a bit agitated if the topic is raised. The idea of purpose often causes anxiety for people.

Be patient with yourself. Anyone who has ever done some soul-searching for their purpose has faced ambivalence and doubt on their journey. Their bewilderment was what prompted them to dig deeper and ask themselves questions, such as, "What am I interested in, what do I care about, and what do I want to achieve?" For some people, the answers come easily, other people feel more ambiguity and can really benefit from working with a coach to get clarity and perspective, and sometimes the answers just take time to reveal themselves. Stay persistent and keep asking questions; the answers will come when you are ready to hear them.

Here are some guidelines that we'll explore in more depth to help you steer yourself in the direction of your North Star:

1. Ask yourself questions about what you want.
2. Believe in the power of one.
3. Accept that you will make wrong turns.

4. Live the life that you want to live.
5. Listen to your heart.

ASK YOURSELF QUESTIONS ABOUT WHAT YOU WANT

*"When what you value and dream about doesn't match the life
you are living, you have pain."*
— Shannon L. Alder

The first thing you need to do to find your North Star is to stop leaving yourself out of your decisions. Stop rushing from one task to another in a mindless haze of productivity, pleasing everyone but yourself. I know far too many people who claim that they don't have the time to focus on their own aspirations or goals. They do. They choose to not *make* the time for themselves. There is nothing wrong with spending all of your waking hours completing a to-do list to satiate other people's needs and convincing yourself that you are leading a responsible life, except that most people who fit that description are unhappy, unfulfilled, and often unhealthy.

Take the time to pause your existing thought patterns and ask (and most importantly, honestly answer) yourself, "What do *I* want?"

I remember when I was planning my wedding and the location was becoming a sticking point with my family. I had some ideas but they were easily overpowered and dismissed by the conflicting desires of some of my family members. The more I tried to appease different people's views of where my wedding should be held, the more flustered and stressed I became. I wanted to make everyone happy but instead I felt like I was failing them. One teary night, I vented my frustrations with my then-fiancé and he asked me, "What do *you* want?"

That question halted my thoughts and overwhelmed me because, the truth was, I had no idea what I wanted anymore. My dreams and wishes had gotten lost in my desire to please everyone else. I had to then put in some conscious and laborious effort to place my desires at the forefront of my mind and bravely ask other people to respect my wishes for my own wedding. It wasn't my family's fault; they weren't "bullying" me into doing what they wanted. The problem was that my ideas were unformed and, while I had proposed some suggestions, I hadn't done so with any true conviction. I was overpowered because I wasn't clear on what I wanted in the first place. Once I was jolted into pausing and reflecting on what my actual preferences were, the whole conversation changed. I gained confidence, I eventually got married in exactly the location of my choice, and everyone was happy in the end.

This wedding location fiasco is an example of a specific situation where my direction was fuzzy because I wasn't considering my needs or wants enough and that lack of clarity led me to feel easily overwhelmed. However, it triggered a chain reaction for me to start focusing on my own desires in other bigger picture ways. Ask yourself the simple question, "What do *I* want?" about specific things, such as where to go for dinner, but then continuously expand it out to bigger picture events, plans, and ideas. Getting clear on your own direction, purpose, and wishes is a matter of giving yourself permission to be heard in your own mind. The more you practice allowing your voice to matter, the more natural it will feel, and the more clarity you'll begin to construct.

I have created a habit of using a "mental checklist" while going about my day to ensure that the decisions I make, both big and small, are truly guided by my North Star. The questions I ask myself aren't difficult, like, "How do I feel about this?" or "Is that what I really want?" but the trick comes in respecting myself long enough to listen for the honest answer. Sometimes the answer screams, sometimes it softly whispers, sometimes the answer has to smack me with a wet fish before I become aware of it – but it is always there.

Become more disciplined with interviewing yourself about your bigger picture and creating your own mental checklist. By learning to habitually listen to yourself about what you really want, and then acting on it, you will command the course of your life.

BELIEVE IN THE POWER OF ONE

> *"The power of one is above all things the power to believe in yourself, often well beyond any latent ability you may have previously demonstrated."*
>
> **— Bryce Courtenay, *The Power of One***

Believe in the power of one. You will never create anything you want if you don't believe in your ability to make it happen.

I once attended a superb weekend retreat that was designed to dent your thinking and ignite change in you. There was one activity we did that I felt was really silly at the time. I had just begun my career shift into public speaking and was not yet feeling confident or competent as a speaker. The activity was to think about your vision for your career direction and dream big, to stretch your imagination into your wildest dreams of what you could achieve. We then had to go onstage and describe what that "dream vision" looked like to the audience. With my heart racing and mouth dry, I stood in front of my peers and recited an imaginary announcement for the "featured keynote speakers at the upcoming 'Influential Women of the Future' convention in Las Vegas." The lineup of speakers included Brené Brown, Arianna Huffington, and Nikki Langman. My peers cheered and threw out words of encouragement, but I didn't believe in what I had just proposed at all. I felt ridiculous imagining myself ever being considered at the same level of influence as Brené or Arianna, who in my mind are like Academy Award winners in the space of personal development.

After that retreat, I pushed toward my North Star. I continued to create content and build a public speaking profile, one baby step at a time. More than anything, I wanted to be a speaker and positively influence many people's lives, so my mission every day became focused on taking the next brave and correct step to put myself out there and get closer to my overarching goal. It took a long time to start feeling results.

When I was training for my first marathon, I didn't feel the gains from my physical efforts with each daily run. I didn't feel like I could accomplish a marathon after completing my first 5k, or 10k, or even half marathon. The goal of being a marathon runner seemed like such a distant target for so long. Most of the time it took an equal amount of effort to keep believing in the dream I was chasing as it did to physically put one foot in front of the other and continue moving.

Beginning a career in speaking felt quite similar. It was only after I persevered in my direction for a while that I could look back and see how far I had come and how much impact I was beginning to have. But I still didn't have the confidence that I would ever have the level of influence as some of the A-listers in my mind. I set my goal of what I could achieve much lower.

One day, I woke up and scrolled through the typical stream of notifications that had come into my social media profiles overnight. There was one notification that floored me. The author of a published article had named a list of people and expressed appreciation for the "personal development experts that were enriching and influencing millions of lives globally." My name was on that list, alongside Brené Brown and Arianna Huffington, and several other celebrities and well-known influencers in the field. I was beyond honored and humbled – I was dumbstruck. I even reached out to the author because I was convinced that was a mistake, but it wasn't an error. It was real. While it might have been one person's determination of who they considered influential at the time, it reignited that moment at the retreat where I doubted my own potential for greatness. It reminded me of the power of one. The power that it takes to believe that you will make a difference to one person can turn into ten people, then turns into one hundred… into one thousand… into one million… into tens of millions.

This author's list of influential experts, and this renewed dream that maybe my name *did* belong next to those other great names, became a new tank of fuel for me on my journey toward my North Star. However far-fetched and absurd your dreams feel, you will be the person who will stop you from getting there by not believing in the power of one.

ACCEPT THAT YOU WILL MAKE WRONG TURNS

> *"Embrace embarrassment. Feeling foolish is part of the path to achieving something important, something meaningful. The more a major life decision scares you, chances are the more you need to be doing it."*
> — **Mark Manson**

Nothing worth having ever comes easily. If you want something, you have to be prepared to take risks, look awkward, be willing to be a beginner for a while, and make sacrifices. You have to overcome your doubts and be braver than your fears. If you think big, listen to your heart, and confidently dedicate your life to following your North Star, you will be unstoppable.

But know this, you will make wrong turns. You will run into roadblocks that you didn't plan or account for. The course of your life is never a straight line. If you get to your destination without any obstacles, your vision isn't big enough. Each obstacle is a stepping stone, an opportunity to build on, and a step closer to your destination.

You may fail. Failure is a natural, and often necessary, part of the process. As when you work out and lift weights, it is the failure of the muscle that makes it possible for the muscle to grow back stronger. You have to be broken down in order to get back up as a more powerful version of yourself.

LIVE THE LIFE THAT YOU WANT TO LIVE

"There is no passion to be found playing small – in settling for a life that is less than the one you are capable of living."
— Nelson Mandela

To be unique is the greatest and simplest thing that you can do. You are you. This is your superpower: nobody else has your experiences. Only a small number of us are fortunate enough to be persevering on the path toward what we actually love doing. We buy into society's version of success and get caught up in the daily grind. Unintentionally, we spend a major part of our life trying to please others and ignoring our own desires. Don't ignore YOU.

Pursue your dreams passionately and with confidence. Live the life that you want to live, have the career you want to have, and don't let anyone knock you off your course. The key to true fulfillment is the joy of being able to do all that you love doing.

Be inspired to be YOU. Dare to be YOU. Do not let the fear of what other people might think dictate your actions. Your life is yours to live.

LISTEN TO YOUR HEART

"You will never be able to escape from your heart. So, it's better to listen to what it has to say."
— **Paulo Coelho**

No matter what choices you make, ensure that you make them because it is what your heart and soul crave. Your heart and soul, not your head, are the guiding forces of your life and it is only you who has the knowledge of your true aspirations. Knowledge that you may not always be mindful of, which often occurs when we get caught up in the hamster wheel of life and we disconnect from our heart. We must be diligent to not let life disrupt what our heart and soul truly want. Nobody has ever dreamed of being a hamster. Listen to your heart and you will know how to follow your North Star.

CHAPTER EIGHT

HOW BAD DO YOU WANT IT? (ACTION)

"The first step towards getting somewhere is to decide that you are not going to stay where you are."

—J.P. Morgan

Having knowledge of your North Star is fabulous, but just knowing where you want to go won't get you there. Without action, direction has no value. Action is the next significant element of the BADASS framework. Everything begins and ends with action. Think about this: there are people less qualified than you, doing the things you want to do, simply because they decided to take action.

When we discuss action as a daily habit of badassery, it's not just about getting things done, it's about getting things done in a strategic and intentional way that yields outcomes. One of the easiest and most abundant ways to take badass action is with goals.

WHY HAVE GOALS?

Direction is pointing the nose of the car down the road you want to travel; action is pushing the accelerator. Goals are the fuel in the tank. Goals give us the energy to take action in a way that gets us to where we want to go. Without clearly defined goals, we become curiously devoted to the trivial and mundane. We lose any sense of direction, progress, confidence, and purpose and can fall into a trap of self-sabotaging behaviors, such as procrastination, blame, indecision, and laziness. Consider that we have 24 hours in each day. If you were to drive your car for 24 hours in one direction you will use approximately the same amount of fuel as if you drove in circles for 24 hours. The difference is, once you have burned that fuel, where are you?

Of course, it is unrealistic to be focused on a goal 24 hours a day, but even with detours and rest stops along the way you will still be closer to your destination if you are intentional about the direction you are driving in. Driving in circles achieves nothing, just like shooting an arrow without a target to hit means you will miss every time.

All successful badasses – entrepreneurs, top-level athletes and high achievers in all fields – set goals. In fact, it's next to impossible to be your most powerful self without having goals to keep you focused. A surprisingly high number of people do not have any goals, which is why they are failing to live up to their highest potential. Start doing the things NOW that your future self will thank you for starting today. Don't fear failure or the unknown. Fear stagnation. As Mel Robbins says, *"Fear being in the exact same place next year as you are today."* Shape your life or it will be shaped for you.

START WHERE YOU ARE

> *"Do what you can, with what you have, where you are."*
> **— Teddy Roosevelt**

Start where you are. You can only start with what you have, not with what you don't have. Don't let not having the ideal set of circumstances be your excuse for not taking action. Opportunity is always where you are, not where you were or where you want to be. All those who arrive anywhere had to begin where they were.

Hamilton Mabie declared, *"The question for each man to settle is not what he would do if he had the means, time, influence, and educational advantages, but what he will do with the things he has."* Don't wait for the perfect time. There will never be a perfect time. Each of us has an ability to create what we need from something that is already here. Sometimes you just have to dare to do it and start taking action because life is too short to wonder what could have been.

CRISIS

Goals can also help you stay focused and sane in times of crisis. I mentioned in an earlier chapter that I was in the middle of my ultramarathon training plan in March 2020 when COVID-19 began to shut everything down. During that time when the bottom was falling out from underneath all of us, sticking to my goal anchored me. Every morning I got up and looked at my training plan that was stuck to the refrigerator door, and asked, "How far am I running today?" It was my source of constant and calm during the storm. I was powerless to change what was happening around me, but what I could control was continuing to take action toward my goal.

Imagine if there was a major earthquake and you were a volunteer rescuer and your goal was to find survivors buried in the rubble. Your focus would be on looking for movement and listening for voices. It's probable that you would still be deeply affected by the scene you were witnessing and the loss of life, but your goal of finding survivors would fill you with the strength, courage, and focus you needed to take necessary actions and minimize the emotional impact of the situation.

Sometimes in the midst of a personal crisis, creating goals or pursuing existing goals, however small, and taking action on them can be your best form of resilience and carry you through the parts of the situation that you cannot control.

HOW BAD DO YOU WANT IT?

Setting a goal or an intention is easy. Achieving a goal can be quite difficult, frustrating, and often causes people to abandon their objective entirely. Why? It's because we go about setting them in the wrong way.

A goal requires three levels of assessment:

1) What do I want?
2) What's my plan to get it?
3) How bad do I want it?

The last question is the most important and the one that will save you a lot of time and strife by answering honestly. If you are fully committed to a goal, you will find all the tools you need to get there – motivation, time, tenacity, and discipline. If you are mostly committed to a goal, you will find excuses.

Asking yourself "How bad do I want it?" will achieve two things. 1) It will show you if you are willing to accept the sacrifices required to reach your goal and 2) it can help you determine if the goal is authentically yours or someone else's goal for you.

For the first part, no reward comes without a price. Are you willing to pay the price to get the reward? This is where you should do your research thoroughly to see what is really involved in the process. It's a nice idea to want to earn a black belt in karate, but do you have a realistic understanding of the amount of training that is involved to achieve that? Go sit with a senpai and ask them how many hours per week, and for how many years, they trained to get to their level. Ask them about their injuries. Ask them what they had to sacrifice to commit to the training. *How bad do you want it?*

> *"One half of knowing what you want is knowing what you must give up before you get it."*
> — **Sidney Howard**

How about starting your own business? How many months or years will you be willing to put in with little financial gains before you start feeling successful? Or if losing weight is your desire, can you visualize what each meal will feel like when you adjust your portion sizes or how you will combat fiercely strong cravings and temptations?

The second part is equally important: Is your goal truly yours? This is where most people get tripped up with effective goal setting. There is a well-established tool for goal setting called SMART. SMART is an acronym that many people are taught for planning goals that are Specific, Measurable, Achievable, Relevant, and Time-bound. It is a wonderful approach for making a plan to get from A to B, however research from the University of Scranton shows us that

92% of people do not achieve the goals they set.[10] The reason is not because the goals aren't SMART. It's because people don't fully own their goals. Your effort level will reflect your interest level.

> *"People aren't lazy, they simply have impotent goals – that is, goals that do not inspire them."*
> ## — Tony Robbins

A classic example of this is people who excel in their jobs, get promoted into management as a reward, and then they fail. Is that because it wasn't their wish to stop doing the job they were good at and become a manager of people? Were they pursuing the wrong goal because someone else told them that the next logical rung on their ladder was management? We do this with other career choices or relationship choices that our soul didn't sign up for because we get pressured or influenced by other people's ideas of what is good for us. We talk ourselves into believing that is what we want, too.

Lead yourself with your heart and then utilize your head. You can't lead yourself with your head and then try to utilize your heart. It won't work that way. The answer to "How bad do you want it?" is in your heart.

I have observed that runners (and most athletes) are cognizant of whether or not something is the right goal for them. For instance, you wouldn't find someone using a marathon training plan and entering marathons if what they really wanted to be was a 100m sprinter. It would be the wrong approach. You know why a runner wouldn't do that? Because they're the ones putting in all the effort! A runner isn't going to bust their butt day after day to follow a training plan for a goal they're not fully committed to hitting.

Why do we get it wrong in other areas of our life? We're still the one putting in all the effort. I constantly see people who are unhappy and unfulfilled because they're pouring tremendous energy into goals that their heart isn't in, and therefore they never accomplish them. On the other hand, knowing that you are lazy or unfocused and therefore not achieving any goals is clearer: it's like sitting in a boat and choosing to not use either of the oars. You know why you are not going anywhere.

However, most people are trying to live a responsible and joyful life by using only one oar. That is heartbreaking. Vast amounts of people spend the majority of their energy pleasing others and going after goals that society has seduced them into believing will create happiness and self-fulfillment, without being fully committed to their own efforts. This illusion convinces them that they are going somewhere and making progress in life while keeping them unaware that they are merely paddling in circles. The result is frustration and discontentment, which keeps us enslaved to searching for external solutions to fill our internal gaps.

I use my approach to running – setting my targets for distances or times that I'm realistically willing to train for – to guide me in setting goals for other areas of my life. When I'm making big decisions or setting career goals, I ask myself, "Is this plan going to get me to a goal that I really want to achieve? How would I approach this if it were a running goal? Would I be happy about putting in the required effort? How bad do I want it?"

THE JOURNEY THAT CHANGES YOU

"What you get by achieving your goals is not as important as
what you become by achieving your goals."
— Henry David Thoreau

When you achieve a goal that is deeply meaningful to you, you will not be the same person that you were when you began that journey. The act of completion is trivial compared to the experience and wisdom gained during the process.

If your goal was to lose 30lbs and you get there, you will have gained so much more than just the thrill of buying new clothes and feeling more attractive. The increased confidence you will have is symbolic of the process you went through, not because of the number reflected back to you on the scale. To lose that much weight you had to make lifestyle choices and maintain discipline and focus for a long period of time. Even if you did go off-track a couple of times, you found a way to navigate your way back on course and that took determination and resolve. You had to resist temptation and hone your patience. You had to stay true to yourself and your goal, even in the face of discouragement. You wanted it bad enough, so you did it.

How many people actually put in that level of effort and make the sacrifices required to lose serious amounts of weight? Not as many as the number of people who set the goal. That's why the journey changes you. A minor part of the reward is the tangible change in your physical body. The journey has gifted you with improved discipline and willpower and confidence that, if you can do this, you can do anything. And that is badass.

The same applies to running a marathon or writing a book or starting your own business. Many people dream about those things, but only a small percentage actually do it. The people that do are changed forever.

> *"It's not the mountain that we conquer, but ourselves."*
> **— Sir Edmund Hillary**

The best result of all is that the person you become after completing a meaningful goal is a person who is likely to achieve future substantial goals. This is why high-performing people in business are often physically fit and have other significant interests, because the actions and skills used to achieve one goal can be applied to another goal, and to another goal. Your self-belief increases dramatically when you know you've got what it takes inside you.

I got sober and have stayed sober; that's the most massive goal I have ever achieved because it took more than 30 years to get there and I continue to treat each day like an accomplishment. In sobriety, I feel like there is nothing I can't do because I am already successful with the hardest thing I can possibly imagine. Running is another self-belief turbo boost for me. When I look at my wall full of medals and what each one represents, the amount of work and sacrifice behind each race, it again solidifies that I am capable of anything that I commit my heart to. That self-assurance spills over to my career success, my speaking, my writing, my ethics, my dedication, my drive, my focus, my productivity, my habits, my relationships, and most importantly my growth mindset.

Success is not what you accumulate, but who you become. As you push your limits, your character develops as a direct result. Therefore, it is critical that we set goals with our heart in charge and do some thorough soul-searching when deciding which goals are the ones we want to commit to – the ones we are willing to go through the storm with and hold onto with all our might. The right goals, the ones you want bad enough, will change your life.

INTENTION VS. ACTION

"What you do speaks so loudly that I cannot hear what you say."
— **Ralph Waldo Emerson**

Here's an inconvenient truth: We judge ourselves by our intentions, but everybody else by their actions. And we, in turn, are judged by our actions.

An intention can't be measured and it means something only to you. Intention shows desire, action shows commitment. Commitment means there are actual expectations in place. Many people are afraid to publicly declare their commitments, because you expose yourself to being held accountable for the action. If you fail to follow through, the confidence others have in you begins to fade. You lose credibility. That lack of follow-through can also be a blow to your self-worth. There is nothing empowering about letting yourself or others down. Over time, if failure to follow through on your commitments becomes a habit, it can lead to self-defeating behaviors and feelings of worthlessness.

Punctuality is not a strength of mine but I am much better at it than I used to be. There was a time when I was chronically late everywhere I went. I was late to work, late to classes, late to appointments, late to social events, and often all on the same day. I disrespected people by keeping them waiting, caused inconvenience, suffered consequences for my actions, and got really down on myself with wicked negative self-talk. But I always had good intentions! I never meant to cause so much upset and seeing other people's frustration caused me a great deal of shame. However, I couldn't change the behavior because I got stuck on my intentions. Intentions are incredibly optimistic; we always imagine the best outcomes when we are hanging on to them. *Next time, there won't be traffic. Next time, the phone won't ring as I'm walking out the door. Next time...*

In order to break my pattern of tardiness, I had to stop investing in my wholesome intentions and take different actions. This was not an easy mission, either. It was a laborious and time-consuming process of trial, error, frustration, determination, and reset to make lasting changes to my time-management. But as it goes with making any change, the pain of continuing to feel like a failure had to become stronger than the risk of adopting the new behaviors. I will never run like a Swiss watch because punctuality is not an innately high value of mine, but I am much better at getting close to the mark now. I don't disrespect people's time or cause as much disruption and that, in turn, raises my self-worth – and self-worth is something that I put a tremendously high value on.

There is power in taking action. When you put motion behind a desire it changes the game. It's both a physical and mental cue that you are in charge now. The only way to influence your own and others' perceptions of you is through what you do, how you show up, and how you follow through. What you planned or meant to do is not important. You cannot be your most powerful self and influence your environment with good intentions alone.

212°

"Inches make the champion."
—Vince Lombardi

There is a fantastic book and video created by Sam Parker called, *212° the extra degree*, that is frequently used or referred to in motivation or personal and professional development contexts. The metaphor is incredibly simple and scientifically sound. At 211° F water is hot. At 212° F, it boils. And with boiling water, comes steam. And steam can power a train. That one extra degree makes all the difference in the world. The same holds true for our actions in everything we do. It's the small things, the extra margin of effort that we put in, that makes a significant impact.

If you want a quick fix or a magic wand to achieve more in your life and ensure better results, it's this: be consistent. The extra degree that creates success is found in the regularity of our actions more than anything else. Consistent effort gives you ownership over your actions and your outcomes. I'm sure you can think of countless examples where this is true. It is not the people who are doing one degree more *once* who win, it's the people who are doing one degree more *consistently* who win. Bruce Lee famously revealed, *"I fear not the man who has practiced 10,000 kicks once, but I fear the man who has practiced one kick 10,000 times."*

Consistency also has a crazy side effect: motivation. Have you ever noticed that once you put something on the back burner it tends to stay there? The back burner is the burial ground for all of the things that once got us energized. I have found that no matter how ambitious I am about achieving something, as soon as I break my routine actions, my motivation flies out the window. And once you have lost motivation, finding it again is like pedaling up a hill from a dead stop – possible, but extremely challenging. Anyone who has ever ridden a bike up a hill can feel the difference between the two in their mind – starting from a fixed position or approaching the hill already in motion.

Consistency of action creates motivation and motivation leads to more action. Motivation is not a precursor to action, as we often like to trick ourselves into believing: It's the loyal result of action. That's not to say that you'll always feel motivated (nobody is motivated all the time), but the ones who want it bad enough know that they just have to keep being consistent and the motivation will come. Start doing, keep doing, do one degree more repeatedly if you want to be great at it, and you are guaranteed to get results.

THE POWER OF CHOICE

"Your life is the sum result of all the choices you make, both consciously and unconsciously. If you can control the process of choosing, you can take control of all aspects of your life. You can find the freedom that comes from being in charge of yourself."
— **Robert F. Bennett**

How often do you fail to follow through on something or give up on a goal you set and justify it with, "I didn't have a choice" or "I couldn't do anything about it?" It's probably more often than you think. The truth is, you ALWAYS have a choice.

It is incredibly liberating to look inward and say, "This was my choice." Then you can accept whatever the situation is and enhance it. When you believe you don't have a choice you assume a victim position.

Let's use an extreme example from Sharmen Lane's article "Choices and Personal Responsibility," to illustrate a situation where one might say they had no choice. Let's pretend you're walking down the street when someone grabs you and holds a gun to your head. They say, "Give me your wallet." You hand over your wallet and the thief runs off. Did you have a choice when you handed over your wallet? Yes, you did. Maybe not an abundance of choices, but you still had at least two. One was to hand over your wallet. The other was to not hand over your wallet. You could say, "True, but if I didn't hand over my wallet, I could have died." Indeed, that could have been a possibility. However, you still had a choice. You chose to hand over your wallet and live versus keeping your wallet and potentially being killed. There were at least two choices. Terrible ones, but choices nonetheless.

So, why do we so often want to hold onto our assumption that we don't have a choice? Is it so we can deflect responsibility, so that the situation is not our fault? So that we have someone or something else to blame or hold accountable?

We can't change other people or circumstances beyond our control, but we can certainly adjust ourselves. It's emancipating to understand that we always have a choice, and we can change our response to anything. No one holds a gun to your head and says, "This is what you must believe. This is how you must act."

The best thing about owning the power of choice is that you enable yourself to take actions that sculpt your life into whatever you want it to look like. And that is powerful.

CARPE DIEM

"There is no better day than today to do the things you have been putting off."

— Hal Elrod

When you procrastinate, you're saying one of two things to yourself, "It's easier to avoid this than to face it" and that's usually incorrect. The other one is "It will be easier to handle this tomorrow (or later)" and that's often false as well. Procrastination is the seed that grows difficulties. When we procrastinate, we never have small problems because we wait until they grow up to address them. Take going to the doctor for a regular check-up as an example. You know you should go, but you feel fine, so you put it off and off and never make that check-up a priority. A few years later you experience pain so you go to the doctor and find out that you have a serious condition that would have easily been detected from a routine exam. Now, you have a big problem that could have been avoided.

Think about things that you have procrastinated on that caused you difficulties. Maybe you had to pay a late fee, worked overtime to meet a project deadline that you knew about for months, lost a lead because you waited too long to get back to the prospective client, or your car ran out of gas. The tasks we postpone never go away, they just become more consuming and urgent the longer we let them grow. The price of procrastination is not always visible right away, either. The true cost is revealed in hindsight. Ask yourself: "If I don't take action now, what will it cost me later on?"

WHY DO WE PROCRASTINATE?

There are many reasons that we procrastinate, and you know a lot of them. How many of the below resonate with you?

Anxiety. Typically, anxiety shows up because what needs to be done seems overwhelming or frightening. Our mind invents a catastrophic story of what "might" happen that is usually blown way out of proportion. We become paralyzed and unable to take action.

Failure. The fear of failure convinces us that it is safer and easier to not try at all than to try and fail. Trying and failing shows courage; not trying at all shows cowardice.

Success. Success is heavy and carries responsibility with it. You might worry about other people's future expectations of you if you do well with this task or situation. Many people unconsciously self-sabotage on the road to success to ensure they don't arrive there.

Perfectionism. Perfectionists tend to take no action if they can't do it perfectly. They restlessly feel a need to research or plan more before they act. Or, they will nearly complete the task but drastically slow down their progress at the end with painstaking attention to minutiae.

Resistance. If you are required to do something that you are uncomfortable with or do not see the value in, you may put it off until the last possible moment or try to avoid doing it altogether.

The most common denominator in all of these examples is fear. Procrastinating is only going to make matters worse. Ask yourself, "What am I afraid of?" and then apply some badass bravery, take a deep breath, and just do it. Many times, if not always, the story we make up in our head is far worse than reality ever turns out to be.

ACTIVITY VS. ACCOMPLISHMENT

A clever way that procrastination disguises itself is through busy activity. Everyone is always on the move – going forward, backwards, or nowhere at all. A common mistake that people make is thinking that the busier they are, the more successful they are. This is a trap. What is imperative is not whether you are hustling but whether you are progressing: activity versus accomplishment.

There was a French naturalist, John Henry Fabre, who conducted an experiment with processionary caterpillars. These caterpillars are understood to blindly follow the one in front of them no matter how they are lined up or where they are going. In his experiment, Fabre carefully arranged them in a circle around the rim of a flower pot so that the lead caterpillar actually touched the last one, making a complete circle. In the center of the flower pot he put pine needles, which is the processionary caterpillar's favorite food. For seven days the mindless caterpillars moved around and around the pot, dying from starvation and exhaustion even though there was an abundance of food less than two inches away. The caterpillars were extremely active, but they were not accomplishing anything.

Humans are different from caterpillars. We have the ability to change our direction and actions anytime we want to. But just because we possess the ability to make different decisions doesn't mean that we do. We often confuse motion with meaning and activity with achievement. We easily get into ruts, which causes dysfunction in our careers, our relationships, or with our health. The ruts can become vicious circles and don't get us any further than those poor caterpillars on the flowerpot. Then we find ourselves resembling the processionary caterpillar more than we would like to admit.

Don't get so busy that you become unaware that you're putting off meaningful goals and lack enough energy to be your most powerful self. If this resonates with you, perhaps one of your urgent goals should be to get better at saying no to "stuff" and yes to yourself.

THE CURE FOR PROCRASTINATION

Here are five actions, inspired by Rick Warren,[11] that you can take to stop procrastinating:

1. **Stop making excuses.** One of the most common excuses is, "When things settle down, I will ..." Things will never settle down to your liking. Make a choice to prioritize what is important and just do it.

2. **Start today.** Not tomorrow, next week, or next month. No one is guaranteed a tomorrow.

3. **Face your fears.** We deny our fears because we view them as a sign of weakness. But fear is a sign of being human, not strength or weakness, just human.

4. **Focus on the gain, not the pain.** The easier the action, the lower the worth. The more difficult the action, the higher the worth. Push through the difficulty and focus on the gain beyond the pain.

5. **Be less busy.** Remember the caterpillars. Don't let your life be so full of activity that you miss out on what you really want.

Procrastination is the cell in which opportunity is locked away. You are your own captor, the one who holds you back from accomplishing more in life by not taking constructive action in the right direction. What price are you paying for procrastination in your life?

NEVER GIVE UP

"The tragedy of life is not that man loses but that he almost wins."
— Heywood Broun

Above all, if you want something bad enough, refuse to quit until you get there. The majority of failures happen when we give up too quickly. Try everything possible: if one approach doesn't work, choose different actions. The more we achieve goals, the easier it is to achieve future goals; similarly, the more we quit, the easier quitting becomes. Josh Billings remarked, *"Consider the postage stamp: its usefulness consists in the ability to stick to one thing till it gets there."* Be a postage stamp.

Badasses are people of commitment, persistence, and endurance. One person with commitment, persistence, and endurance will accomplish more than a thousand people with interest alone. Don't let your starting point – how much money, ability, or equipment you are starting with – become your excuse for procrastination. Just start with a million dollars' worth of determination. Remember: it's not what you have, it's what you do with what you have, that makes that extra degree of difference. Success with anything is ultimately a dance between perseverance and action.

No matter what, remember this simple math formula that will always work for you on your road to self-mastery: multiply your commitment, divide your distractions, subtract your excuses, and add action.

CHAPTER NINE

THE GREATEST LOVE OF ALL (SELF-LOVE)

"You can search throughout the entire universe for someone who is more deserving of your love and affection than you are yourself, and that person is not to be found anywhere. You yourself, as much as anybody in the entire universe, deserve your love and affection."

— attributed to Buddha

When I developed the BADASS framework, this was the section that I contemplated the most. All of the other letters were quite clear to me. Originally this letter of the acronym was self-belief. Believing in yourself is a necessary ingredient in beginning to tap into your most powerful self. Self-belief allows us to honor our unique skills, knowledge, abilities, and worth. Self-belief motivates people to explore their potential and this impetus may lead to the achievement of goals and aspirations. Self-belief is incredibly important, *but it's not enough.*

So, I changed the letter "S" to Self-respect. Self-respect encompasses all the components of self-belief, but it also embraces self-care and how we demonstrate outwardly that we want the world to treat us. Practicing self-care is a cornerstone of self-respect because these are the habits and behaviors that prioritize being considerate of yourself. You need to be in charge of monitoring your own needs – such as sleep, nutrition, exercise, work/life balance, and stress levels – as no one else can do this for you. When you treat yourself this way, you send messages to your conscious mind that you believe you are valuable and worthy of respect, and that others should see you this way too.

By contrast, if you regularly work yourself into the ground, drain your resources, neglect your physical and emotional needs, or engage in other unproductive behaviors, your subconscious understands that you are only valuable insofar as you can do things for others and your needs don't matter. Others will observe the way you treat yourself and, instead of respecting you, they will learn how far they can push you.

In addition to self-care, self-respect also means that you take responsibility for your values, beliefs, and behaviors. Your actions reflect your core values, you comfortably show people your authentic self, you respect your environment, you honor the commitments that you make to yourself, and you set and enforce boundaries with others. Other people will mirror the amount of respect you show yourself. Confucius advised, *"Respect yourself and others will respect you."* Self-respect is supremely important, *but it's not enough.*

After a lot of deliberation and looking to my heart for the answer, I became aware that the first "S" in BADASS is Self-love. Self-love is the key to your overall wellbeing. It includes all of your feelings and beliefs about yourself and your value, how you treat yourself, and what you project to the world, so it encompasses self-belief and self-respect. It's also much, much greater than that. Self-love involves unconditional acceptance and ownership of your whole self. That means being in a committed relationship with every single bit of you – the good, the bad, and the ugly – and not just selecting the good parts and disowning the stuff you'd rather not see. That involves work and dedication and is not an easy relationship to be in because the process of self-discovery and self-acceptance is lengthy and arduous, but the rewards are profound and infinite.

Self-love is the glue that holds the BADASS framework together – it's the glue that holds you together, too:

- It takes tremendous **bravery** to actively confront and love parts of yourself, but it takes **self-love** to be willing to be brave and face your fears in the first place.

- **Authenticity** demands that we are truthful to our whole self. **Self-love** allows us to access the self-compassion we need to authentically own our complete self and the courage to show our uncensored self to others.

- **Direction** motivates us to prioritize self-love because without purpose and meaningful goals we can get easily lost in feeling like we exist for the benefit and disposal of others. **Self-love** helps clarify purpose because only our heart knows our true aspirations and can lead us in the right direction.

- It takes tremendous **action** to intentionally love ourselves because being truly self-aware and benevolent toward ourselves is not something that just happens; it's a commitment that involves time, energy, and active focus. **Self-love** promotes action because when we take conscious steps toward prioritizing our needs and wellbeing it creates the space for us to be available for others and actively pursue our passions and goals.

- And lastly, what we cover in the second "S," your current **self-talk** is a direct reflection of your existing self-love. When our **self-love** guides how we talk to and think about ourselves, it can have staggering benefits to our confidence, focus, career, relationships, and overall well-being.

Self-love is the whole package. We can get by and have a satisfying life by "liking" and projecting parts of ourselves, but true power – deep, core-shaking power – can only come when we fully embrace and practice genuine self-love. Self-mastery is built on the foundation of self-love.

NO THANKS, NARCISSUS

"We are wont to condemn self-love; but what we really mean to condemn is contrary to self-love. It's that mixture of selfishness and self-hate that permanently pursues us, that prevents us from loving others and that prohibits us from losing ourselves."
— Paul Valéry

The commonly held belief that loving yourself is narcissistic and therefore bad, is false, so it's time to get over it. This limiting belief will serve no purpose but hold you back. On the surface, the story of Narcissus seems to demonstrate that loving yourself is arrogant and indicates a pompous disregard for the needs of others. But, upon deeper inspection, Narcissus didn't love himself, he loved a reflection of himself. Narcissus was actually incapable of true love in any form, especially the love of self. In fact, it is feelings of anguished inferiority and overreliance on others' approval that drives narcissistic behavior in the first place.

When self-love is insufficient, a person can use attention-seeking tools like flattery, charm, extreme helpfulness, and impressing others with their achievements and inflated attributes to secure the reflected images of themselves that they crave. Because they require a constant supply of attention and adoration to fill the gaps that their lack of self-love leaves, they don't have the capacity to be self-aware, demonstrate empathy, and fully love others. Eventually, they are left with self-loathing and loneliness because the demand they place on others to compensate for their impaired self-love becomes exhausting and intolerable.

There is a diagnosable condition called narcissistic personality disorder, but it is not to be confused with respect, care, compassion or belief in our own worth. In fact, we are all prone to acting in narcissistic ways from time to time. Feeling hurt, invalidated, or rejected in either subtle or overt ways can cause mental pain and blur our self-perception. This can lead to a dependence on other people's opinions, judgments and interpretations of us to correct our feelings – which makes us vulnerable to being manipulated or potentially being manipulative ourselves. There is nothing inherently wrong with this tendency: it's simply a part of the human condition and it's useful to acknowledge that we are all susceptible to this type of behavior on occasion. The danger in overreliance on others to meet your internal needs is that it's erratic; everyone else you encounter will have needs of their own to fill, too, and are likely to be seeking some sort of validation themselves.

When authentic self-love is present, we don't demand the approval of others to feel valuable. We can appreciate receiving an endorsement, but it doesn't send us into a damaging spiral if we don't get it. Self-love allows us to accurately evaluate ourselves, esteem ourselves from the inside, and maintain a fairly consistent perception of our worth no matter what happens externally.

WHAT WILL OTHER PEOPLE THINK?

> *"Care about what other people think and*
> *you will always be their prisoner."*
> — **Lao Tzu**

Even if our behaviors or emotional responses aren't as extreme as complete dependence on other people's perspectives to feel okay with ourselves, we do put importance on what others think of us – to some degree, most of the time. Do you ever:

- Deliberate over what to wear to the gym?
- Apply makeup to go to the grocery store or pick up the kids?
- Worry after the meeting about all the things you should, or shouldn't, have said?
- Think you were "too loud" at the party? Or not funny enough?
- Take six selfies to get just the perfect angle?
- Feel like others judge your health habits by what's in your grocery cart?
- Modify your personality or "put on a front" at work or in social situations?
- Feel insecure in a bathing suit?
- Apologize if your car or home is messy?

- Feel rejected if your LinkedIn article or Facebook post doesn't get many likes?

Chances are you probably relate to at least one of these examples or can think of a few of your own. All that happens when we preoccupy our minds with other people's possible interpretations of us is that we judge ourselves harshly. We feel uncomfortable in our own bodies. We want to apologize for being ourselves. We put in extra effort to meet our estimation of other people's standards, which is usually inaccurate. We feel phony, anxious, critical, not good enough, not likable enough, not smart enough, or not attractive enough.

The truth is, other people's opinions of us are not something we have any control over. Their assessments have nothing to do with us and everything to do with them, their past, their judgments, their expectations, their insecurities, their preferences, and their dislikes. This can be hard in practice, but to have robust self-love we need to learn how to care a bit less about what others think.

A couple of effective ways to train your mind to place less importance on what other people think are to remember your goals (Chapter Eight) and your values (Chapter Six).

STICK TO YOUR AUTHENTIC GOALS

Remember, one of the most important questions we can ask ourselves when setting meaningful, authentic goals is, "How bad do I want it?" In addition to the two benefits discussed in the previous chapter, a third benefit to this question is that if the goal is truly something your heart desires, you will be more resilient to negativity from others about it.

Frank was a client of mine who made the decision to leave his corporate job in sales and become a photographer. Even though he was making a substantial income, he wasn't happy and had enough of "swimming with the sharks," as he put it. He faced a lot of criticism about this decision from his friends and former coworkers, and especially from his wife. His wife's feedback was fear-based about their financial security, so Frank understood where she was coming from, but it wasn't enough to make him change his mind. The tension nearly ended their marriage. But Frank wanted it badly enough, so he turned the energy of opposition into motivation to prove to the naysayers that he could pursue his passion of photography and succeed. He did.

Frank's niche in photography is shooting landscapes. At first, he relied on selling his artwork to bring in income, but found that wasn't enough. So, he started a landscaping business. With a pick-up truck and a few pieces of equipment, Frank started maintaining most of the residential gardens in his area. That gave him supplemental income and more control over the quality of the landscapes in his photographs. He is now featured frequently in real estate and gardening publications and his business is in such high demand that he has hired two part-time assistants. Naturally, the negative chatter died down around him and it was largely because he fully believed in his goal. Even when other people dismissed his idea as "stupid" and "sure to fail," Frank wasn't deterred. He loved photography and was willing to take a huge gamble and endure negative feedback to pursue his passion. In effect, Frank honored his self-love by staying true to a goal that was authentically his.

Frank recalls one of his favorite quotes from Pablo Picasso: "My mother said to me, 'If you are a soldier, you will become a general. If you are a monk, you will become the Pope.' Instead, I was a painter, and became Picasso." Frank held onto the belief that he cóuld be his own version of Picasso, but he had to ride the waves of judgment first and force himself to put less importance on what other people's opinions were.

KNOW YOUR VALUES

Keeping your values in the front of your mind is a brilliant way to overcome the seeds of doubt that creep up when we are faced with rejection or opposition. When you are unclear on what's really important to you, you can feel a lack of confidence and get easily pushed around by others opinions, viewpoints, and beliefs. However, when you are firm in why something is significant for you, it provides you with strength to withstand resistance.

I put high value on clear and concise communication. I remember an instance once where I was given a large task by my boss that was quite vague. No due date, no method of work, no indicator of how much time I was expected to spend on it, etc. Naturally, I took a list of clarifying questions back to my boss and he got irritated by my detailed probing. I privately understood that his annoyance was because he didn't know most of the answers and this project had been haphazardly pushed off to me. Nonetheless, I persisted and requested that he investigate some of the details or put me in touch with someone who could. He liked that idea even less and started to fire back by saying things like, "If you don't think you can handle it, I'll ask someone else to do it for you" and "This is ridiculous, you have a brain, use it."

Comments like that might have thrown me off-course with insecurity and worry that I was being a nuisance if I hadn't been so grounded in my values at that time. Instead, I met his curt tone with an even voice and replied, "If this project is important to the business, it's worth doing accurately and to a high standard. To me, that means having the correct information up front. I am happy to do the research myself, if you will kindly point me in the right direction. If not, then perhaps it doesn't actually need to be done?" Knowing my value of clear and concise communication going into that conversation allowed me to stand in my own power and honor myself by not allowing my boss to push me around. His words, although cutting, didn't have a lasting effect on me as a result.

When you make a decision to do something, and hear those nagging voices of doubt and apprehension get louder, think about what you value to quiet them down. If you value efficiency, keep that in mind instead of your appearance when you rush to the grocery store or do school pick-up. If you value determination, focus on that when you feel unfit inside the gym. If you value quality family time, put your attention on building sandcastles with your kids at the beach instead of being preoccupied with your "imperfect" bikini body. Your values are your heart's compass and they will surely steer you clear of the danger of what other people think.

REDEFINING SELF-CENTEREDNESS

> *"If you aren't good at loving yourself, you will have a difficult time loving anyone, since you'll resent the time and energy you give another person that you aren't even giving yourself."*
> — **Barbara de Angelis**

Let's talk about the term "self-centeredness." If you look it up the meaning of it, you will be met with an array of unsavory adjectives such as: egocentric, egotistical, self-absorbed, concerned solely with one's own interests, engrossed in self, etc. At face value, it's quite an antagonistic label. We have been socially conditioned to resist being perceived as self-centered. This is especially true for women and, the more successful a woman is, the harder it is for her to escape public judgment and criticism. I know many successful women, or women who are on a journey of defining their own success, who understand and relate to the fear of being perceived as self-centered. Understandably, men don't want to be poorly categorized either, but our culture offers a wide berth of forgiveness for the stereotypical responsibilities of a man. For everyone's benefit, we need to redefine what self-centered actually means.

A center is a core and having a strong center or core is desirable, in just about any context. When we think about the physical body, your core is what provides your body with the most strength. It takes the load for many activities that you perform and keeps you upright. In physics, the center of gravity is thought to be where the concentration of weight is held and what creates the most stability. In tall buildings, aside from the foundation, the building's core (usually composed of the stairwell and elevators) is the strongest and most reinforced portion of the building. In the game of chess, the center is the most important part of the chessboard. Having a "strong center" is a configuration where the opponent can't pressure, attack, or disrupt the pieces or force them to move.

No matter how you assess it, the notion of having a strong center is extremely positive, unless we're talking about ourselves – then, it becomes negative. We have to look at that differently. We must view ourselves as the core of everything, and everyone, in our lives and strengthen ourselves first. If the core is weak, it weakens everything that surrounds it. If you are not whole, all you can possibly give are pieces. When you invest in yourself first you have more wealth to give to those who depend on you.

When I practice self-love – live by my values, pursue my purpose and goals, set boundaries, and care for my physical health – I become a much better parent, wife, friend, leader, and business partner. By creating abundance in myself first, I have more physical and mental capacity to support others. Practicing self-love and making your needs your first priority is not selfish, it's self-full. When your cup is full, you have more to give. When you constantly put others' needs before your own and don't fill your own cup, that's self-less. When your cup is empty, you have less to give.

Frequently, some individuals become *people-pleasers* who are afraid to be authentic or take care of themselves first. Guilt stops them from putting any priority on themselves. Their mental boundaries are closely enmeshed with others' because they were raised to take care of others and neglect themselves. We often see this pattern handed down from generations. While there might be some merit in our grandparents or great-grandparents choosing to sacrifice their own physical needs, such as eating a meal, to ensure that others were fed, this is rarely the case anymore. Today, it's more commonly emotional neglect that people practice based on beliefs that were handed down to them that self-suffering demonstrates care and love for others.

If this pattern resonates with you, please understand that you are not alone and it's not your fault. You are likely just modeling behavior that you were taught. But think about what example you are setting for your future generations. I don't believe there are many parents in the world whose intention is to say, "My child, I'm going to show you how to neglect your own needs so that you grow up to be burned out, unhappy, overweight and on medication for most of your adult life." This might be a harsh example, but it's sadly more common in the Western world than the amount of people who are demonstrating what self-respect, goals, values, and healthy self-centeredness look like.

Changing patterns and long-held beliefs is laborious, so turn the tables one rotation at a time. Perhaps start with one goal and ask others to support you with that goal. I know people who run races and put their training plan on the refrigerator or somewhere that the whole family can see it and ask the others to help keep them accountable. Kids love holding their parents to task. Doing this allows the parent the permission to have time to themselves while they train and demonstrates goal setting, planning, execution, and self-care at the same time. Another idea is to get up earlier. That's not always the most desirable option for some, but it works. If making time for yourself feels unachievable with all your other commitments, schedule time at the beginning of the day. An extra five or seven hours a week of pure focus on you can make a very big difference to your overall wellbeing.

CASTING A SHADOW

"Filling the conscious mind with ideal conceptions is a characteristic of Western theosophy, but not the confrontation with the shadow self and the world of darkness. One does not become enlightened by imagining figures of light, but by making the darkness conscious."

— Carl Jung, "The Philosophical Tree," ***Alchemical Studies***

As previously explained, genuine self-love demands that we own our whole self, not just the appealing bits. Everyone casts a shadow. In Jungian psychology, the "shadow" is the part(s) of ourselves that we either don't like, try to disown, or are entirely unconscious of. According to Jung's theory, we psychologically distance ourselves from impulses, emotions, and thoughts in ourselves that we find undesirable or inferior. Things like judging others, criticism, rudeness, a sense of entitlement, jealousy, arrogance, or biases and prejudices can all exist in our shadow. Rather than engage with parts of our ugliness, our mind dismisses them and pretends they don't exist. However, we cannot get rid of them, so they become repressed into our unconscious: our darker side, the shadow that always looms behind us.

Seeing our own shadow is arduous and formal "shadow integration" work is painstaking and unpleasant, so it's not a popular undertaking (although I highly recommend it). Only a select few who are completely committed to the pursuit of self-mastery will venture into those thorny bushes. However, we are experts at identifying shadow traits in others. In fact, our culture thrives on it. Look at the success of the celebrity gossip industry.

HOW CAN I RECOGNIZE MY SHADOW?

One of the most effective ways to become aware of your shadow is to recognize when you have a strong emotional charge to something or someone, a reaction like someone just touched a live wire in you or "pushed your buttons." If you are in a workplace or a group situation, observe the way other people respond to the same thing/person. If you are significantly more bothered than others, it's probably a shadow thing. When you have that strong emotional charge, what you are actually experiencing is an emotional attraction. It may look and feel like an aversion, but that qualifies as an attraction (like a magnetic pull) because our attention becomes attracted to the thing that bothers us and we focus on what we don't like.

To assist you with understanding your shadow better, consider who you are (negatively) attracted to and what they do that affects you, such as:

- Who causes you to feel like nothing you do is ever good enough?
- Who causes you to feel like it's always your fault?
- Who really annoys you or pushes your buttons?
- Who do you complain about?
- Who disgusts you?

These people and behaviors that you just identified; they are your triggers. They are also now your teachers because whatever characteristics we choose to deny in ourselves, we see in others. This is called "projection." We project and magnify onto others what we conceal within us. First, we reject, then we project.

Identifying triggers and projection can be a difficult process due to our natural desire to avoid acknowledging the shadow self. Saying things like, "HE procrastinates, badly. I don't procrastinate at all, I'm ALWAYS prepared in advance" are common because if you have repressed that trait in yourself, it probably won't be immediately visible.

Also, people commonly look for "apples for apples" first, such as, "His monthly report is late every single month. Mine is never late." However, the reason why your coworker's procrastination bothers you so much may not have anything to do with your own behavior in the workplace. Maybe it's the boxes of your late mother-in-law's belongings that have been stacked in your garage for the last three years (that you feel guilty about ignoring) that is nagging at your subconscious and coming out as annoyance with a coworker's faulty behavior. Or perhaps it's not related to a tangible action at all, but rather a fear you have that you are not acknowledging.

I worked with a client once who was annoyed by her ex-husband's inability to plan ahead. They had a shared custody arrangement and she felt she was doing all of the legwork on organizing the kids' school and sports schedules with both parents' work and life commitments. She felt exasperated that he often had "last minute" things come up and wasn't appreciating her efforts to make the arrangement fair for everyone involved. She had a difficult time seeing beyond that anger because she was comparing her actions to his actions, which were indeed unbalanced. After a bit of work, we concluded that her anger was not in response to anything she was or was not doing herself, but rather an unconscious fear that she would "drop the ball" somewhere. As a working single parent with multiple external responsibilities, she felt overwhelmed by the number of things she was trying to manage and the fear that she would somehow forget something or let someone down led her to behave in tightly controlled ways. Once we shifted our focus onto that fear and the resulting behaviors, it became apparent why perceived disorganization and laziness in someone else caused her to fume.

Asking yourself questions about why you are triggered by certain events or people can be challenging and frustrating, like looking for the correlation between the "loud, opinionated guy at work who interrupts all the time" and something that you are repressing. Exploring your shadow with a coach or other professional is a good idea because they can ask you some objective questions from an untriggered perspective to help you see the links that might be hidden to you.

THE BENEFIT OF SHADOW INTEGRATION

Integration, in Jung's definition, means that we identify the source of the psychological triggers (e.g. the repressed fear, pain, greed), stop rejecting these parts of ourselves, and integrate them into our conscious everyday lives. The aim is not to defeat our shadows but to accept them, seek to learn from them, and use them as productive fuel. Fear becomes an incentive for bravery. Pain an impetus for resilience. Aggression transmuted into grit and drive. We can't correct undesirable behaviors until we deal with them head on. Through the integration, the shadow's previously rogue power is diffused, and true wholeness can be attained. True wholeness is true enlightenment.

When you work to integrate your shadow, you may find that you live with increased self and other awareness, thereby becoming more conscious of your own needs and those of the people around you. The awareness acquired from the integration engages our emotions, which in turn informs our decisions, actions, and interactions with others. We develop a greater capacity for empathy and compassion as well by understanding how and when others get triggered themselves.

You build trust in your relationships, and the people whose lives you influence might then influence others, building even more healthy relationships. Even random acts of kindness to strangers could increase the likelihood that they will be kinder to strangers in turn, which may lighten the mood of a community overall. You hold within you the power to activate a surge that will vibrate through the lives of the people around you. Doing deep inner work may feel like a self-absorbed process, but you'll come to find that, at its core, it truly becomes about so much more than just you.

IT'S YOUR STORY TO TELL

"Owning our story and loving ourselves through that process is the bravest thing that we will ever do."

— Brené Brown

You have a story in you, and it's a beautiful story. It's a comedy, it's a tragedy, it's poetry, it's prose. It's a sad story, it's a happy story, it will have you gripping the edge of your seat, and howling with laughter. The characters are vibrant, there are exquisite moments that will take your breath away, unforgettable triumphs, heart-wrenching failures, and many, many lessons learned.

You can't erase any of the previous chapters, but that's okay. They were written exactly the way they were supposed to be written, and they're perfect. But today's page is blank and so is every page for the rest of the story. You have full control over how you write your present and your future. At this moment and for all the rest of the days of your life, you are a BADASS. You are Brave, you are Authentic, you follow your Direction, you take Action, you practice Self-love, and you speak empowering Self-talk. Everything you need to write your masterpiece is in your hands. You can write it in whatever way you want. That is your power. Nobody can take the pen away from you. It's your story to tell. But please, however you decide to write it, make sure it's a story about unconditional love.

Loving yourself through your successes and celebrations is easy. Loving yourself through your missteps, fears, and inadequacies takes a bit more effort. We often mistake self-love for conditional self-like. Instead of authentically demonstrating self-love and acceptance, we evaluate ourselves on a scale of worthiness. When we are good, we reward ourselves with love and approval. But when we are bad, we punish ourselves by stripping away our permission to feel love. We become the harshest castigator in our lives.

You must unequivocally feel love for yourself no matter what your circumstances are. You have to love yourself as you are today; at your current address, at your current job, with your current possessions, at your current weight, and with your current relationships. And until you can love yourself unconditionally, your love for another will always be conditional.

When you love yourself unconditionally you accept all parts of you and appreciate your shortcomings as something that makes you unique. There is a practice in Japan called "Kintsukuroi" which means "to repair with gold:" It's the art of repairing broken pottery by filling the cracks with gold. It is believed that when something has suffered damage and has a history it becomes more beautiful. Love yourself in this same way. Love your cracks and your flaws. Create your own gold lacquer out of self-compassion, forgiveness, and gratitude. For, when you tenderly take your broken pieces and mend them with grace, you will undoubtedly become stronger and more beautiful. Grace is the sine qua non of self-love.

CHAPTER TEN

YOU GOT THIS (SELF-TALK)

"Man often becomes what he believes himself to be. If I keep on saying to myself that I cannot do a certain thing, it is possible that I may end by really becoming incapable of doing it. On the contrary, if I have the belief that I can do it, I shall surely acquire the capacity to do it even if I may not have it at the beginning."

— **Mahatma Gandhi**

The final component of the BADASS framework is to critically examine your Self-talk – because whatever you tell yourself you are, you will become. The words you speak about yourself, to yourself and to others, have the power to construct your entire life in a desirable or undesirable way. Self-talk is a natural flow-on from Self-love because how we speak about ourselves reflects the love we honestly have for ourselves. If we were to analyze the messages we tell ourselves, they're not generally filled with self-love unless we're intentional about that. Quite often we believe that we are actively practicing self-love only to be surprised by how defeating our unconscious communication actually is. If there were a mental recorder on your thoughts for a 24-hour period, I bet you'd be astonished at the percentage of positive, enforcing, or inspirational thoughts you have versus the amount of negative, defeating, or sabotaging thoughts you have.

Some people have famously mastered the art of self-talk and simultaneously exhibited tremendous bravery, showed unwavering authenticity, had unmistakable direction, took massive amounts of action, and unquestionably believed in themselves to become everything that their words proclaimed that they were. They are badasses in every way, who know how to access their most powerful selves and have enjoyed enviable success as a result.

Take Muhammad Ali as an example. He insisted, "I am the greatest" but he didn't just say that once. He repeated it all the time. He declared it publicly. He whispered it to himself. He roared, "I am the greatest" long before he became, arguably, one of the greatest boxers in history. Will Smith joked about his early career and ascent to fame, "In my mind, I've always been an A-list Hollywood superstar. Y'all just didn't know it yet." As a struggling young entertainer, Jim Carrey reportedly wrote himself a check for the amount of $10 million for "acting services rendered" and dated it 1995. He carried that check in his wallet for ten years to fuel him with inspiration. In 1995, Carrey was cast in the movie *Dumb and Dumber* for a fee of... you guessed it, $10 million. J.K. Rowling, Oprah Winfrey, Denzel Washington... There are so many examples of mega-successful people who credit a lot of their prosperity to their unshakeable belief in themselves and their positive self-talk. This is not a new idea. Many religious and philosophical teachings throughout history have been rooted in the idea that our thoughts will manifest into our reality.

My relationship with the "badass" concept originated with self-talk. Long before I developed the acronym and framework, I said the word badass to myself a lot as a noun. I have always associated a positive meaning to that word and defined a badass as someone who shows strength, determination, grit, and a desire to be the best at what they do. That definition was exactly what I needed to build self-confidence in times where belief in my own abilities faltered. Like many others, I'm no stranger to self-doubt. I struggled tremendously through the years to achieve lasting sobriety, so I became steadfast in repeating to myself, "I am a badass. I got this. I can do this." I questioned some leaps of faith in my career direction and when I would stall mid-air, I got right on my internal bullhorn and shouted, "Come on, badass, you got this!" In my journey as a runner, I have felt endlessly discouraged and frustrated when my ability couldn't keep up with my ambition and I've applied soothing layers of compassionate self-talk such as, "You're a badass, Nik. Keep going, you will get there." I dish out dozens of badass messages throughout the day every day, sometimes more if the situation calls for it, to consistently reinforce my internal thoughts. It all boils down to one simple idea: I am what I tell myself I am.

Find a word or phrase that empowers you and develop a habit of using it. Align yourself with that word or phrase and make it your personal theme. Tattoo it to the inside of your forehead. Feel free to use the word badass or choose a different noun or adjective that suits you better, but whatever it is, make sure it's consistent. We know our actions have to be regular to get results; similarly, our mental processes and self-talk have to be dependable, too. So, think you're a badass. Tell yourself you're a badass. Tell other people that you're a badass. And guess what will happen?

NEGATIVE MESSAGES

"A mind filled with negative thoughts makes you feel miserable and inadequate and will lead to failure after failure no matter how hard you try to succeed."

— **Steve Backley**

Negative messages surround us everywhere we go: They are inescapable. We are saturated with negativity in our schools, our workplaces, our families or social structures, and all the various forms of media and social media. Not only is it all around us, but negative messages are the fastest moving form of any kind of communication, especially on social media. Studies have shown that the reposting volume of negative social media messages is 1.2x - 1.6x that of positive and neutral messages.[12]

This is damaging in the long run, because these external negative messages leave lasting impressions on our minds, influence our perception of the world around us, and can drastically impact how we feel about ourselves. Negative messages fuel negative self-talk, which creates a negative mindset. We must be very cautious that we do not shackle ourselves to a negative mindset and instead, intentionally steer our self-talk towards positivity and optimism.

What you invite into your life and the messages you choose to absorb are determined by your recurring thoughts and the beliefs you have about yourself. Positivity attracts more positive outcomes and experiences; negativity attracts more negative outcomes and experiences.

AFFIRMATIONS

"Nothing binds you except your thoughts; nothing limits you except your fear; and nothing controls you except your beliefs."
— Marianne Williamson

Every thought you think and every word you say is an affirmation. An affirmation is simply an assertion that something is true. Affirmations act directly on our emotions and feelings and the more they are repeated, the more they are interpreted by our subconscious as fact. That means, whenever you think a negative thought about yourself or make a disparaging comment you are actually affirming that as your personal truth. Your subconscious mind accepts your commands as reality because it can't tell the difference between what you tell it versus what is objectively true. For example, when you say to yourself, "I'm not disciplined… I never stick to my goals… I'm always going to be fat… I'm not likeable… I'm not good with money…" your subconscious doesn't argue with you, it just accepts that as truth.

This is also where we fall victim to "confirmation bias," which is searching for what you want to see. Rather than looking at all data objectively and possibly seeing information that conflicts with your existing belief, you seek out information that supports what you already believe to be true. For example, if you believe you have a double chin, you are going to scrutinize what your chin looks like in every photo you see of yourself to confirm, and then reaffirm, that you indeed have a double chin. Or, if you don't believe you are a good salesperson and a coworker sold twice as many units as you did again this month, you might interpret that as supporting evidence that your sales skills are terrible and continue to affirm that belief.

Luckily, the exact same is true for positive thoughts and affirmations. Positive affirmations help us to literally change the neural pathways in our brains. Neuroscience has taught us that the brain has an ability called "neuroplasticity" – essentially, the brain is able to reprogram itself and change over time. Just as we do repetitive physical exercise to get stronger, repeated affirmations can be thought of as exercise for our mind. Learning to think differently is part of how we learn to get rid of negative pathways and replace them with new circuitry in our brain. Positive affirmations help us to challenge and defeat self-sabotaging thoughts and stop bad habits – and negative self-talk is a terrible habit that we need to break.

Positive affirmations are typically constructive, optimistic statements that we compose or that others have created that resonate with us. We can use the same statement for long periods of time, like a personal mantra, or vary them from day-to-day. Both techniques are successful. Here are some examples to start with:

- "I am a badass."
- "I am strong."
- "I am resilient."
- "I am likeable."
- "I am smart."
- "I am taking steps to achieve this goal."
- "I am confident."
- "I am prepared for this."
- "I am stronger than temptation."
- "I trust my training."
- "I deserve this."
- "I am worthy of this."
- "I got this."

You will notice that the word "I" appears in all of these statements, they are written in the present tense, and they are short and powerful. Do not overcomplicate an affirmation. Be specific, brief, and include action words or feeling words. The perfect affirmation is "I am _____."

Importantly, always frame your affirmations positively. The unconscious brain does not process negative words, such as "no" or "not." This means that the statement "I am not afraid to stand up for myself" is heard as "I am afraid to stand up for myself." Instead, say "I am confidently standing up for myself."

Depending on your personal preference, you might choose to elaborate on your affirmation to keep you motivated and dreaming big like, "I am sailing out of the harbor on my new catamaran." If that works for you, by all means expand on the statement so you can feel yourself taking the action.

My style, thus my recommendation, favors moving forward in incremental steps. When I was just starting to run, my focus was on quitting smoking and being able to run 5km. If I had told myself, "I am a marathon runner" at that time it would have been too far-fetched for me to sink my hooks of belief into and I would have felt really silly and inauthentic. It might have even had a counterproductive effect and I would have stopped saying it – and maybe given up trying to run altogether. But if I had repeated things like, "I am a non-smoker" or "I am a runner" that would have been more palatable and I would have been able to buy into those beliefs. Now that I have a few years of running confidence under my shoelaces, I am able to stretch my affirmations to my next level of goals and say, "I can run a 100km race." I know I can run 60km (37.28 mi), so I believe that I have the capability to, and will soon, accomplish 100km (62.14 mi) and more.

THE NEUTRAL ZONE

"There is nothing either good or bad,
but thinking makes it so."

— **William Shakespeare**, *Hamlet*

Now that we've looked at the damaging effects of negative self-talk and the benefits of positive affirmations, let's explore a third option – neutrality. Many people might appreciate the evidence that supports flipping all of their negative thoughts into positive ones but, like my marathon runner example, feel artificial saying words that they don't actually believe. So, let's throw in a compromise and allow a neutral zone.

But first, you cannot claim that you are incapable of transforming *any* of your current self-sabotaging beliefs into positive affirmations. There have been many points in my life where I struggled to feel positive about anything, where the weight of depression and addiction was like a thick, heavy blanket of smoke hovering around me. But even in those dark times I was still able to find some things to reframe in an optimistic way. Sometimes that was simply changing, "I'm never going to get through this" to "I will get through this." Maybe I couldn't see *how* that was going to happen, but I was able to grasp onto at least a sliver of hope that things could improve. If that's all you can do, that's good enough. So, be optimistic where you can and develop positive affirmations around those areas of optimism.

Sometimes we have negative beliefs that are so deeply ingrained that optimism doesn't feel like a realistic option at all. That's where the neutral zone comes in. A neutral thought is something you already objectively agree is true and that expresses a more measured, impartial belief about yourself. It's not as empowering as a positive thought, but it's also not counterproductive. Plus, it's a step up from your current negative thought. Over time, thinking neutral thoughts will strengthen your confidence so that you can comfortably upgrade to positive thoughts.

Here's an example of a neutral thought:

Current negative thought: *I am so fat.*
Neutral thought: *I have a woman's body.*

Replacing the words "I am so fat" with "I have a woman's body" is an easy first step because, assuming you are indeed a woman, having a woman's body is something you would objectively agree is true. Stay with that thought for as long as you need to until you have stricken the "f-word" (fat) from your internal vocabulary and are consistent with saying to yourself that you have a woman's body. You don't need to attach any sentiment to the thought at this point, it's not important how you *feel* about your woman's body, just that you have one. The next step is to turn the neutral thought into a positive affirmation that feels manageable, and continually raise the bar and stretch yourself, such as "I am making good food and exercise choices that are helping me to lose 5lbs." Once you've lost 5lbs, create a new affirmation about losing the next 5lbs, or stretch yourself to envision losing 10lbs. Once you can go from negative to neutral to positive, then just keep building more positive stepping stones. You'll become more sophisticated at fine-tuning your affirmations over time and more adept at using them for a variety of issues and goals.

THE RETICULAR ACTIVATING SYSTEM (RAS)

If you want to know what your life will look like a year from now, pay close attention to the messages you tell yourself today. You create your future in your mind with your current thoughts, feelings, beliefs, values, direction, actions, and goals. You do this without even being conscious of it. Your thoughts about yourself in the present moment, coupled with your thoughts about your future self, get fed into your subconscious programming.

All of your thoughts about your future self are not only active in your subconscious thinking, they are also mediated by your Reticular Activating System (RAS). The RAS, which is a bundle of nerves at your brainstem, serves as an information filter and takes instructions from your conscious mind and passes them to your subconscious mind.

Because of this biological function, whatever you consciously focus on will be filed away in your subconscious mind with a note to reappear in the future. The RAS is the reason why you can be talking about buying a yellow car and then suddenly it seems like the roads are full of yellow cars. The RAS helps you organize information by sifting through millions of pieces of data in your brain to filter out unnecessary stuff and makes sure the information that's important to you gets through. In other words, it gets rid of the white noise. Hence, you were talking about yellow cars, so therefore the RAS assumes yellow cars must be important to you. Your RAS will sift out the insignificant bits so that you become more consciously aware of the yellow cars on the road.

The RAS is designed to support you favorably. In the same way that it filters and organizes important data, the RAS seeks information that validates your beliefs. It filters the world through the parameters you give it, and your beliefs shape those parameters. The RAS helps you see what you want to see and in doing so, influences your actions. Focus on the bad things and you will invite negativity into your life. Focus on the good things and you will likely find them, because your brain is seeking them out. It's not fate, luck, or Murphy's law;

it's your Reticular Activating System showing you the world as you have indicated you want to see it.

This is why it is so important to have consistent positive affirmations. When we have empowering thoughts, words, and images always in the front of our mind, they become our "keywords." The RAS is our search engine. There are millions of websites, but if we type in a keyword, our attention will be drawn to the sites that support that keyword.

VISUALIZATION: WHAT YOU SEE IS WHAT YOU WILL BE

"When we visualize goals as complete, it creates a conflict in our subconscious mind between what we are visualizing and what we currently have. Our minds are hard-wired to resolve such conflicts by working to create a current reality that matches the one we have envisioned."

—Jack Canfield

Words are incredibly compelling and the words you choose when you talk to yourself will change your life for better or for worse. Guaranteed. But there is another level that you can add for a double punch of potency: Visualization. Your unconscious thinks in pictures and visualization feeds the RAS the pictures it needs to filter the information effectively. The most powerful affirmation or message you can send from your conscious mind to your subconscious mind is a visualization or mental image.

Your RAS also does not have a bullshit detector: It cannot tell the difference between reality and imagined reality. This advantage is frequently used as a high-performance hack, such as athletes using mental rehearsal methods where visualization of their performance can stimulate actual performance in real time conditions. Similarly, imagining failure and seeing yourself fail in your mind will pave the way for actual failure because your brain assumes that's the desired outcome. This is also why worrying about things you can't control is a massive waste of time and energy. When you worry, you effectively program your mind to ignore the variables that will benefit you and direct your attention to the things that can possibly go wrong but you won't have any influence over anyway.

When we encourage positive cognitive reframing and visualize ourselves succeeding at a task or completing a goal, we produce feelings of confidence and familiarity. Take crossing the finish line of a marathon, getting a standing ovation after a performance, or facilitating a difficult conversation, for example. If we play that scene over and over in our minds and couple it with feeling the emotions that we would expect to feel at that time, when it comes time for that event to happen in real life our brain is prepared and in charge because it's thinking, "We know exactly how to do this, we've been here a hundred times before!"

I read a story recently about a man who had both of his arms amputated and was awaiting delivery of his new modified car. He was excited for the newfound independence that having his own car would bring, but he was terrified of how it would feel to actually drive it. He had seen the modifications demonstrated: His left foot would operate the steering device while his right foot would operate the gas and brake pedals. To calm his nervous anticipation, he visualized that demonstration over and over and imagined it from the first person, as if he were looking down at his own feet executing the motions. When he took his first actual test drive, it felt completely natural to him like he'd been doing it for years, and erased all of his brewing anxiety.

LIGHTS, CAMERA, ACTION!

Now, visualization and positive affirmations are fabulous and will elevate you on your road to self-mastery, but the sugar in the recipe is action. If nothing changes, nothing changes. We can play a mental movie with an amazing script all day long, but intentional and focused effort will guarantee that we maximize our returns. Plus, the more action you take that is in line with your goals, the more your RAS will work for you by bringing forward the information that will help you succeed.

Here's a few gold star ideas to help you get the most out of visualization and affirmations:

1. **Be clear on your what and why.** There is little benefit in visualizing hitting the target if you aren't sure what you are aiming for. Spend some time refining, condensing, and crystalizing what you actually want and what your motivation is (your "why"), then visualize smashing the bullseye.

2. **Understand what kind of learner you are and work with your natural style.** If you are an **auditory** learner, repeating positive affirmations out loud – not just in your head – will solidify the messages for you effectively.

   If you are a **visual** learner, you might really lean into seeing images of yourself or things you want in different locations/ situations and having written reminders. This is where something like a vision board or writing down goals and affirmations and putting them in places where you see them (sticky notes, screensavers, mirrors, etc.) can be powerful visual stimulators.

If you are a **kinesthetic** learner and thrive in environments where you can touch or do things, look for ways you can reinforce your positive messages in action. I'm predominantly a kinesthetic learner so if I am trying to learn or remember something, like practicing a pitch or presentation, I will pace the floor while I am rehearsing out loud.

However, most of us are a combination of learning styles (there are more styles, but these three are the most common) so if we can hear, see, and touch a message, we increase its power significantly. For example, when I am intending to get out the door for a run but my motivation is like a wet sandbag, I will say out loud, "Come on, badass! You got this." Then, I will look at my wall of medals and walk over and hold one in my hand. The weight of the cold metal transports me back to when I received it and the feelings of pride and elation that I felt. That process is enough to lift my game at that moment and get me out the door. Quick motivation hacks like that work most of the time to propel me into action. I say, I see, I touch, I do.

3. **Surround yourself with inspiration and positive influences.** We are all influenced by our environment, in some good ways and some bad ways. Every moment of your life you are absorbing information, so make a conscious effort to be selective with what you take in. Decide what inspires you and cultivate the people, information sources, places, and activities that are aligned with that inspiration. Make sure that the people you invite into your life are the type whose qualities, passions, and perspectives are in line with your highest goals and dreams.

EXPECT **BADASS** RESULTS

Visualization and affirmations allow you to transform the beliefs and expectations you have about yourself. Coupled with action, the way you think about yourself will influence your motivation, habits, and put you in control of your outcomes. If we harness this power properly, it can lead us to develop deep confidence in ourselves and unbridled mental strength.

Visualize what you want from your life. What does your life one year from today look like? Take some time to really answer that question. Think about it long and hard and map out every precise detail of the person you want to be this time next year. Know exactly where you want to go and put your focus on getting there. If it feels comfortable, repeat this process with a three-year vision – who are you three years from today? Then go for a seven-year vision. I once had a mentor who advised me to set my long-term goals seven years out. I asked, "Why seven?" She replied, "Because five years isn't long enough and ten is too far away." That made sense to me and ever since I have worked on a similar logic of one-year, three-year, and seven-year plans.

When the components are fused together, the BADASS framework is a formula for success. Practiced daily, it is a key that unlocks your most powerful self. Over time, it is a roadmap to self-mastery. Apply it frequently and in generous doses.

Ask yourself, "How big is my **brave** today?" in all that you do because it is in overcoming our fears, great and small, that fills our tank with confidence – and confidence knows no limits.

Be **authentic** every day and remember that we lie the loudest when we lie to ourselves. Never compromise who you are, or be less than you are, for anyone. Some people won't like the authentic you. That's okay. They're not your people. As Dita Von Teese famously proclaimed, "*You can be the ripest, juiciest peach in the world, and there's still going to be someone who hates peaches.*"

Make it a priority to follow your true **direction** and ensure that your heart is your lamp, guiding you along your path. Know where you are going and why. John F. Kennedy maintained, "*Effort and courage are not enough without purpose and direction.*"

Take **action** toward your goals every day. Herculean efforts are not required; consistent and deliberate daily action will get you to the finish line skillfully – just like the story of the Tortoise and the Hare. Put in one degree more effort every day if you want to be exceptional and, no matter what, don't give up on yourself.

Self-love is wealth and owning, accepting, and caring for your whole self is the greatest investment you'll ever make. Many people like themselves, or parts of themselves, but only a few embrace and unconditionally love their whole self. Be one of the few. There is no self-mastery without self-love.

And finally, be in control of your **self-talk** because you will become what you tell yourself you are. If you don't intentionally talk to yourself with love and conviction, yourself will talk to you... and it probably won't be gracious. To be a completely masterful and powerful badass, remember the words attributed to Buddha, "*What you think, you become. What you feel, you attract. What you imagine, you create.*"

CONCLUSION

When I initially disclosed my intention to write this book, some people were horrified that I wanted to be so publicly honest and forthcoming about my struggles and failures. *Why would you do that? Why would you lay yourself open to judgment and criticism? What if someone tries to discredit you?* And, my favorite... *Do you really want your son to know his mother is an alcoholic?* My answer to that last question was a resounding yes. The most precious gift I will ever give to my son is to demonstrate what overcoming your own battles looks like, how to get back up when life kicks you in the teeth, how to be accountable for your choices, how to be unapologetically authentic, how to show up every day like a badass, and how to never, ever compromise how powerful you are or stop believing in yourself. That's the most valuable gift I can give to anyone, and that's exactly why this book needed to be written.

Success is not owning multiple properties, collecting degrees from the most prestigious schools, or seasoning your resume with high-powered corporate positions. Those things might help you feel successful, but true success comes when we have maximized every opportunity to love – ourselves, the people we hold dear, and the world we live in. Success comes when we recognize our brilliance, embrace our potential, and confidently stand in our true power.

True power is not actualized by hiding from adversity. True power does not come from allowing fear to guide you on a leash. True power comes when you look fear square in the eye and say, "I'll take my chances." You don't see risk-averse people summiting mountains, and kid, you've got mountains to climb.

For me, it took the threat of death and sinking to the depths of despair countless times to wake up to my own power. But even then, I struggled to feel like I had a story worth sharing. I had heard countless inspirational stories from people who had overcome major adversity but I held onto a limiting belief that something out of your control had to happen *to* you to be considered worthy of an influential story. I didn't believe that hope and inspiration could be gleaned from someone whose prison was of their own making. Shame wanted to keep me small and tell me that my story wasn't good enough. I chipped away at shame and over time I began to see that it's not the events that made the difference – whether it was a shark attack, child abuse, a debilitating illness, being paralyzed in an accident, or self-destructive behaviors. In fact, some of the most powerful stories I have heard were not based on dramatic events at all. It is not how misfortune is presented that motivates others, it's the recovery. There is no genius in getting knocked down, the inspiration is in getting up. It is not how big the beast that entertains, it's the bravery of the warrior that draws the crowd.

The road to fully owning and accepting my whole self has been paved with broken glass at times but it's been the most worthwhile adventure I've ever been on. And through the process, I've learned how to make peace with shame and embrace my own value.

Now, I dedicate my energy to leading others on their own journey of self-mastery. There are many tools I use to drive the charge through that storm, but mostly, I inspire others by the way I have learned to lead and love myself.

When I first started calling myself a badass people thought that was cute and didn't take much notice, like, here was this little chihuahua barking about how strong and powerful she was. But I kept barking and now the big dogs sit down. You will be whatever you choose to be: It's up to you to decide how much impact you want to have on yourself, your environment, or the world. That doesn't mean that the world should be full of dominant leaders, far from it – that would be a crowded and unproductive platform. Sometimes the most effective people are the ones who have the power to change one heart. But you will never influence anyone else until you influence yourself first.

I hope you are proud of who you are – even if you aren't exactly where you want to be. I hope you accept that you have to live the content first before you can tell the story. I hope you remain steadfast to the vision of where you are going. I hope you find what you are searching for. I hope you forgive others for the things they weren't able to give to you. I hope you forgive yourself for the things you wanted to give and weren't able to. I hope you discover that most of what you need is already inside of you. I hope you learn to fall in love with the discovery process, with the messiness of it all.

I hope you value every step you take for the rest of your journey. It may not always feel enjoyable, but learn the lessons and never lose the ability to be optimistic. Celebrate the little things for a macro-win is nothing more than an accumulation of micro-wins.

Treasure your micro-wins. I hope you believe in the potential you have. It's much greater than you imagine. I hope you give yourself permission to be your most powerful self. If you aren't confident with how much potency you truly have, just remember that it only takes one match to create an explosion. I hope you know how much you will inspire others.

Every day that you show up in the world as a badass, you influence others. Simply striving to be your most powerful self will motivate others to upgrade their own efforts. Even when you don't feel like it, keep going. You never know who you are affecting along the way.

Above all, I hope you inspire YOU.

ABOUT THE AUTHOR

Nikki Langman is an International Speaker, Author, Thought Leader on Emotional Intelligence and Self-Mastery, Business Consultant and Facilitator, and Endurance Runner. She is passionate about personal transformation and self-leadership and believes that our potential for impact and influence with others is dependent on how effectively we understand and lead ourselves first.

Nikki speaks at events, schools, sporting groups, and conferences globally on the topics of self-mastery, resilience and overcoming adversity, emotional intelligence, nonverbal communication, and leadership.

As a Business Consultant and Facilitator, Nikki is committed to guiding organizations to achieve higher, sustainable levels of business excellence. She has led successful emotional intelligence and leadership programs for many global organizations with exceptional results in executive and team leadership, personal empowerment, culture enhancement, and significantly improved workplace safety.

Nikki is an Accredited Practitioner of Genos Emotional Intelligence Programs, DISC ADVANCED® Profile System, and LEGO® SERIOUS PLAY® Methodology. She holds a Bachelor of Arts in International Business from the University of California, Irvine. A native of Orange County, California, Nikki lives in Melbourne, Australia with her husband and son.

REFERENCES

1   D'Arcy Lyness, "Cutting," KidsHealth, 2015, https://kidshealth.org/en/teens/cutting.html

2   "What is Meth Cut With?", 2020, American Addiction Centers, https://americanaddictioncenters.org/meth-treatment/cut-with

3   "Overview of Eating Disorders Today," 2019, Family Talks Clinic, https://familytalksclinic.com.au/predicting-psychosis-brain-folds-hold-the-key/

4   Art Van Zee, "The Promotion and Marketing of OxyContin: Commercial Triumph, Public Health Tragedy," Am J Public Health, 99(2) (2009): 221-227, doi:10.2105/AJPH.2007.131714.

5   ibid.

6   National Institute on Drug Abuse, "Opioid Overdose Crisis," 2018, https://www.drugabuse.gov/drug-topics/opioids/opioid-overdose-crisis

7   ibid.

8   Berterame S, Erthal J, Thomas J, et al. Use of and barriers to access to opioid analgesics: a worldwide, regional, and national study. Lancet (London, England) 2016;387:1644-56.

9   Leon F. Seltzer, "The Force of Your Anger is Tied to the Source of Your Anger," Psychology Today, 2018, https://www.psychologytoday.com/us/blog/evolution-the-self/201807/the-force-your-anger-is-tied-the-source-your-anger

10 University of Scranton, Journal of Clinical Psychology, 2012

11 Rick Warren, "Stop Procrastinating," Ministry Today Mag, 2013, https://ministrytodaymag.com/leadership/preaching/19937-rick-warren-stop-procrastinating

12 Sho Tsugawa and Hiroyuki Ohsaki, "Negative Messages Spread Rapidly and Widely on Social Media," (2015): 151-160, 10.1145/2817946.2817962.

CPSIA information can be obtained
at www.ICGtesting.com
Printed in the USA
BVHW091333120521
607050BV00006B/1256